Overcoming Teen Depression:
A Guide for Parents

Overcoming Teen Depression

A Guide for Parents

Dr. Miriam Kaufman, BScN, MD, FRCP

FIREFLY BOOKS

A FIREFLY BOOK

Published by Firefly Books (U.S.) Inc. 2001

Second Printing

U.S. Cataloging-in-Publication Data
(Library of Congress Standards)

Kaufman, Miriam.
    Overcoming teen depression : a guide for parents / Miriam Kaufman.
[272] p. : cm.
Includes bibliographic references and index.
ISBN 1-55209-520-7 (pbk.)
1. Depression in adolescence. 2. Depression, Mental. 3. Parent and teenager. I. Kaufman, Miriam. II. Title.
616.85/ 27 21   2001 CIP

First published in the United States in 2001 by
Firefly Books (U.S.) Inc.
P.O. Box 1338, Ellicott Station
Buffalo, New York, USA
14205
www.fireflybooks.com
Published in Canada in 2000 by Key Porter Books Limited.

Electronic formatting: Heidy Lawrance Associates
Design: Peter Maher

Printed and bound in Canada

Contents

Acknowledgments

I would like to thank my friends and colleagues who gave me articles from their files or suggested where I could get good information: Peter Rumney, Gary Remafedi, Karen Leslie, Paul Steinhauer and the Sparrow Lake Alliance, Anne Griffiths, Ed Blackstock and Irena Sakova, and Jim Deutsch.

Catherine Moravac, Wendy Melnik and Roberta Benson were all helpful in the data collection and classification stage.

Stan Kutcher was kind enough to read the manuscript. He sent me what he referred to as a "short note"—five pages of encouragement and suggestions. This was much appreciated.

Les Fleischer, Bonnie Heath and Sharon Nancekivell also read the manuscript and made a number of helpful comments.

None of these people are responsible for any mistakes in this book.

Barbara Berson at Key Porter helped me through the rough spots, often acting as a sounding board when I was struggling with issues of style. Wendy Thomas and Doris Cowan were of great help in editing the book. I hope the job gets easier for Wendy as I learn more about the craft of writing with each book.

As always, Roberta, Jacob and Aviva put up with my

inattention to them during the process of writing. Their love and encouragement was always important.

I started writing this book in an ICU waiting room. I would like to thank my father, Nathan Kaufman, for surviving so beautifully. He and my mother, Rita, and my siblings, Naomi, Michael, Hannah and Judith, were supportive and giving throughout the creation of this book.

Introduction

"I know what you can do for your book: ask any teenager to tell you what they think of their lives." This somewhat cynical comment about teens and depression comes from my 15-year-old son. Many people think of adolescence as a time when angst, sadness and despair are normal, and the rebellious or disturbed adolescent has always been a familiar character in books, plays and movies—as long ago as the time of the ancient Greek tragedians and as recently as the latest Winona Ryder film.

Movies, books and common wisdom aside, adolescence is not usually a morass of mental illness. Although several studies have shown that, overall, the mood of teens tends to be lower than that of younger children (that is, they are sadder), and that adolescents are more aware of their emotions than children, the majority of young people get through adolescence without major problems.

But during these developing years, many teens *will* experience at least one bout of major depression. Exactly how many young people go through such an episode is difficult to determine. Studies vary in how they define depression—and whom they ask: teens often say they are depressed, while their parents, asked about their son or daughter, say their kids are doing fine. However, it is probably fair to say that fewer than 3 percent of teens are experiencing a major depression at any given time. Three percent may sound low, but that means that in every high school classroom there is probably one teen with a major depression. Another way of putting it is that 15 to 20 percent of teens will have a diagnosable depression at some time during their adolescence. Mild to moderate depressive symptoms are found at any given time in up to 35 percent of teens.

What exactly do we mean by depression? As defined by therapists and doctors, it is a complex blend of emotional and physical symptoms and behavior. From a medical point of view, depression always includes depressed mood, but this might be difficult for a teen to put into words. She may not describe this as feeling sad, but more as lacking feeling. Deep despair is another description that some people give of how they feel. The writer Sylvia Plath described the sensation of a bell jar descending around her, making the world seem remote, not really touching her.

Most depressed people describe a lack of enjoyment in life (anhedonia). A depressed teenager may notice that things that made him very happy before pass without notice now. He may observe others around him enjoying themselves, but he cannot join in with the feeling, although he may still participate in the activity.

Other feelings are associated with depression. One of the most common is a feeling of worthlessness. A teen may talk about not being able to do anything right, or about not being worthy of love, affection or respect. Maybe she tolerates abusive behavior from a friend or romantic partner because she does not think she deserves any better. It could be that she is feeling guilty about things that weren't her fault, were relatively minor or were even imagined.

A number of physical symptoms are part of depression. There may be a change in appetite, often decreased appetite. Although in adults a typical problem associated with depression is early-morning awakening, teens are just as likely to sleep more than usual, or to have difficulty both falling asleep at night and waking in the morning. Fatigue is a common problem for depressed people, including teens.

It is very worrying for parents if, along with a depression, the teen frequently thinks about death. This may not be thoughts about suicide, but could involve dwelling on thoughts of people who have died, on events involving death that are reported in the news, or on theological questions about death and the afterlife. Suicidal thoughts or attempts are a clear indication that the teen needs help immediately. Chapter 11 discusses suicidal thoughts, feelings and attempts in more depth.

Such a wide variety of sometimes contradictory symptoms may be confusing. A depressed teen may say that he is sad, or he may not. He may eat too much, not enough or the same as always. He may sleep more or less than usual, or not change his sleep patterns. He may seem hyperactive or sluggish. He may ask for help, or angrily reject it. All of the major types and subtypes of depression, and the available treatments, are described in this book.

Readers will quickly notice that, except for the question-and-answer section in Chapter 12, which has a section devoted to teens, this book is addressed primarily to parents. I expect that the majority of readers will be parents. Depressed teens often don't have the energy to read or even to go out to a bookstore or library to get a book. Also, many of the chapters are based on questions that parents have about depression. Teens often have only a few questions—"When will I feel better?" "Why do I feel so awful?" and "Will these medication side effects go away?" Of course, any teen who wants to learn more about depression is welcome to read about it here! There are no parental secrets in these pages. As much as possible I have tried to look at the available literature in all the areas I discuss. I have indicated where there is research to support what I say.

For many reasons, your teen may not want to get help for depression. Maybe you think she's depressed, but she doesn't think she is. Maybe she isn't depressed. She could be so depressed that she can't imagine that anything would help her. She might have other reasons to be suspicious of health care providers. Unless she is suicidal, you cannot force her to get help, but you can be encouraging and supportive. You can also help by researching treatment options and by presenting some choices to her. You may even want to ask her to read a chapter in this book. Above all, be persistent in your offers of help.

My hope in writing this book is that it will be useful to both teens and parents who find themselves in this difficult situation, and to teachers, guidance counselors and other people who work with adolescents. Much of the information comes from my own and my colleagues' experience, the rest from the available medical and psychological literature.

The effects of adolescent depression are never restricted to the teen. Family, friends and others may also be profoundly influenced. And just as you are affected, you can help. Parents are especially important to teens, even though teens may not admit it. Parents can help teens get better by helping them find treatment, by supporting them, by being willing to listen and in many other ways. Remember to always have hope. Although teen depression presents a major challenge to everyone in the family, it can be overcome.

1. What Exactly Is Teen Depression?

To parents, a teen's depression can seem like a storm that has blown up suddenly, almost overnight. Here are Aisha's parents:

She's 17 now, and it seems like only yesterday she was a happy, outgoing child, full of affection and jokes … now she's withdrawn, and doesn't seem interested in the things she used to care about. She looks tired all the time, and sometimes I can tell she's been crying. I've tried to talk to her, ask her what's wrong, but she just says she doesn't know. She's always had her quiet moments, but usually she was cheerful—or we thought she was.

She seemed depressed after her boyfriend split up with her. We figured that she would feel better after a while, but two months later, she still wasn't calling friends or going out with them. She came home right after school and spent hours in her room. She didn't seem to be eating well, and we suggested that she get help. Aisha didn't seem enthusiastic about getting help so we put off making any decisions about the situation for a month to see if she'd begin to feel better. When nothing changed we called our family doctor for advice. She told us Aisha might be seriously depressed and advised us to get therapy for her.

The Medical Definition of Depression

"Major depressive disorder" (or "clinical depression") as defined by therapists and doctors, is a group of symptoms, not a single feeling. We call a combination such as this a syndrome, that is, a group of signs and symptoms that occur together. For a patient to be diagnosed with a syndrome, a number of these problems must occur together, but it is unusual to find all the problems associated with a syndrome in any one person.

The characteristic symptoms of depression always include a feeling of unhappiness ("depressed mood"), but this feeling may be very different in different people. Some people describe it as sadness, others as numbness, emptiness or a feeling that nothing has any meaning, that nothing is quite real. Activities that once pleased or excited the depressed person are now uninteresting.

Nothing seems to be worth doing. The depressed person is often listless and has no energy, and may feel that she is worthless, and doesn't deserve to be happy anyway. Feelings of guilt are common: she may blame herself for things she has done or failed to do, or dwell on her belief that no one likes her and she will never succeed at anything.

Physical symptoms, sometimes referred to as "vegetative signs," can also signal depression. The teen may not feel like eating and may avoid coming to meals with her family. Parents may not notice this, especially as teens have many reasons to be out of the house at mealtime, or may say they already had a snack. Busy schedules can mean that families eat together infrequently. You may only recognize your teen's appetite change when you see that your teen has lost weight. On the other hand, some depressed teens have an increased appetite. This too can be difficult to detect, as teens going through a growth spurt will also eat much more.

Sleep problems are also typical of teens but feelings of

fatigue can be found in depression, even in teens whose sleep patterns have not changed. Related to fatigue is a feeling of being slowed down. The teen may feel as if she is pushing her way through something heavy and resistant, describing it as being "like moving through a sea of honey." One patient said it was like the feeling she had in dreams sometimes, of running on a beach but never getting anywhere. However, other teens complain of feeling agitated and having trouble sitting still. You may notice your teen pacing or jiggling.

Depressed teens commonly have problems concentrating, both at school and elsewhere. Your teen may find that he does fairly well in activities that are easy and automatic, such as playing familiar computer games, but that he has more difficulty performing new tasks or anything that requires sustained problem solving.

For parents, the most frightening development is their daughter or son talking about suicide. A teen who is expressing suicidal ideas needs help immediately. Chapter 11 discusses suicidal thoughts, feelings and attempts.

Not all depressive symptoms are related to clinical depression. They may not even be part of the same spectrum of events. It can be difficult to predict which "blue" teens will go on to have a significant problem.

A diagnosis of major depression will be made if the depressed person's feelings of sadness, or consistent loss of interest or pleasure, have gone on for at least two weeks, and if four of the following six difficulties have occurred almost every day: appetite problems; sleep problems; lack of energy; feelings of worthlessness, hopelessness or guilt; difficulty concentrating; suicidal thoughts or attempts. Suicidal thoughts do not have to occur daily to be included in this list. Remember that what you and your doctor are watching for is a pattern of changes in a teen's usual behavior, sustained over a couple of weeks or longer.

Teen Depression Is Different from Adult Depression

Joan went to see her doctor because of sleep problems. For a number of months she has been sleeping very badly. She finds it hard to fall asleep, but usually manages to get up at her usual time to go to school. "Sometimes I feel like a zombie for half the day," Joan says, but by evening she's revved up and unable to fall asleep again. Joan's doctor told her that he thought she was depressed. Her mother thinks the doctor must be wrong. She herself had a few bouts of depression, when she "just sat around the house all day." She didn't have the energy or the desire to get together with friends, but since Joan still goes out every weekend and spends hours on the phone, her mother doesn't believe she can be depressed.

Teens appear to have a somewhat different experience of depression than adults. From her own experience of depression, Joan's mother defined depression in a way that excluded her daughter's symptoms. But teens can sometimes muster more energy for social interactions than older people. In fact, they may even seem to draw energy from a situation that would drain a depressed adult.

Depression in a teen can even affect growth and development. Puberty may be delayed, especially if the teen is not eating enough. The teen who has already started her periods may find that they become irregular when she is depressed, or they may be more painful.

Abstract thinking skills and the ability to concentrate are both negatively affected by depression. Although this is also true of adults, teens' thinking abilities are constantly called upon and evaluated at school, so there can be major, early repercussions such as school failure. Difficulties with problem-solving may make it more difficult for the teen to seek help or to benefit from it.

Teens are at a stage of life in which major changes are not only possible but inevitable. They are used to change and may therefore be able to recover from a depression and its effects more completely or more quickly than an adult. This is not to say that depression in teens is a passing stage that doesn't need to be addressed, but rather that adolescence is a window of opportunity for personal growth. Teens may also be more willing to believe that things have improved sooner than an adult would, perhaps because they have had less experience of failure and disappointment, and thus have less on which to base a gloomy outlook.

It can be difficult for teens to talk about what they are feeling, especially in the early stages. (In this regard, they are no different from adults.) Unlike an adult, who has had previous episodes of grief or depression, a teen may not even realize that she feels sad.

Adults often feel embarrassed about being depressed, as if they have done something wrong. This is much more rarely the case with teens, who seem to view a depression as something that has descended on them, or as someone else's fault.

Even Children Get the Blues

Sam is only 12 years old and yet his teacher thinks his problems at school could be due to depression. He seems to be "off on another planet." His previously excellent memory seems to be failing him, or maybe he just doesn't care enough to get things right. His teacher is not sure which it is, but she thinks he should see his family doctor about this. Sam's parents want to help, but they find it hard to believe that someone this young, who isn't even showing signs of puberty, can be depressed.

Even young children can become depressed and sometimes suicidal, although this is not common. Sam is entering a vulnerable age—the likelihood of becoming severely depressed increases dramatically in adolescence—and it is very possible that he is depressed.

There are a number of theories why teens are more prone to depression than younger children. One is that "depression genes" might be turned on at this time, either because the genes are somehow programmed to do so (like a time bomb), or as the result of changing hormone levels. Hormone levels themselves have been postulated as the cause of depression. However, age is more clearly linked to depression than the stage of puberty that has been reached; a 14-year-old who has not reached puberty is (for example) on average more likely to be depressed than a 12-year-old who has.

Another theory is that more negative life events occur during adolescence than in earlier life. Certainly there are many difficult transitions during this time, such as the move to high school, and more potential for loss, as grandparents age and die, romantic relationships end and families move.

Some people feel that younger children don't get depressed as often because they have less ability to think about the future and, therefore, are less capable of feeling hopeless. Hopelessness is the one feeling that is almost always associated with depression.

How Do Depressed Adolescents Actually Feel?

Paul is a fairly cheerful adult. He has no memory of being unhappy when he was a teenager ("I was having too much fun," he says) and he usually tends to see the bright side of a situation. He is having trouble understanding what his depressed daughter

*is going through. It seems to him that she has no "real" reason
to be sad.*

Depressed people feel more than sadness. They feel fear, inner-directed hostility, shame and guilt. No matter what age you are, sadness is often the result of loss. This might be what Paul would consider a "real" loss, such as a pet dying, a friend moving away or a prized possession being broken. The loss may also be less tangible, like losing your role as the smart kid in the family, or a sports injury interfering with your goal of becoming regional champ. We are usually sad about things that have already happened, whereas the anticipation of the same losses more often evokes fear or anxiety. Anger about a loss may turn into sadness when we become resigned to the loss.

Feeling an emotion can have many effects. When a person is sad, his memory is poorer and he has difficulty taking in new information. It has recently been suggested that this may be a positive effect; the sad person is freed to concentrate on his sadness and its cause, as he is somewhat unable to perform other physical and mental tasks. In this interpretation, depression, like physical pain, is a sign that something is wrong—a sign nature makes as unpleasant as possible so that the depressed person won't ignore it. (This theory is unproven—and controversial.) The theory also suggests that happiness stimulates a higher level of interest and satisfaction in performing tasks, thus enhancing problem-solving skills and bringing back memories of good times, presumably making one feel even happier. If your teen can feel happy sometimes, it doesn't necessarily mean that he is feeling better in general, but the occasional cheerful mood may help him get better.

Emotions can be generated as a result of an external stimulus (feeling angry as a result of someone's behavior, feeling happy when your team hits a home run) or they can be internally generated (thinking about happy or sad occasions, making the facial or body gestures that go with an emotion), and there are times when they just seem to come out of the blue. This is often the case with depression.

Girls, Boys and Depression

Gender differences in depression are easy to see. (The physical and political aspects of these differences are discussed in greater detail in Chapter 13.) We often hear girls talk about being depressed and about their friends getting treatment for depression, but boys rarely discuss such things. It's not surprising that most people think that depression is more common in teen girls than in teen boys, although physicians and therapists sometimes wonder whether depression rates aren't really the same for males and females; the only difference appears to be that boys are reluctant to talk about their feelings, thinking that "real" men don't get sad, they only get angry or resentful (see Chapter 13).

In childhood, males and females have equal rates of depression. Although very young boys seem to be more likely to become depressed than very young girls, by late childhood the numbers for both sexes are equal. Then, in adolescence, a real gender difference appears: the proportion of girls with major depressive disorder begins to rise; among adults the number of women who suffer depression is double that of men.

Boys and girls also experience depression differently, according to studies. Boys are more likely to report feelings of agitation, whereas girls report feelings of fatigue. Boys may be less likely to come right out and say they feel sad. Their less "traditional" symptoms may lead a parent or health care practitioner away from wondering about depression and to focus on anxiety (see Chapter 8) or a condition known as attention deficit disorder. This possibility supports the argument that the gender split is due to underdiagnosis.

Some researchers think that part of the increase in depression in girls in particular is related to increasing levels of female sex hormones. Other symptoms would support this, including irritability and depressed mood occurring before menstrual periods, complaints of depressed mood in women on the birth control pill, and an increase in psychiatric disorders in women after childbirth. However, arguing against this theory is the fact, noted earlier, that rates of depression in teens seem more closely linked with age than with pubertal levels.

Other Symptoms of Depression

Sandy has some of the typical signs of depression, such as seeming sad and crying often, but she also exhibits other worrisome behavior. Her parents are very concerned that she doesn't appear to be interested in her friends anymore, not even in her boyfriend.

In addition to the "defining" symptoms of depression discussed above, teens may tell their parents about a number of other feelings, physical symptoms or changes in behavior. Many of these symptoms are pairs of seemingly opposite things.

Frequent crying spells are common in depressed teens. These may go on for a long time and be impossible to stop until your teen is "cried out." Non-depressed teens also seem to cry more often than younger children, but these spells are usually shorter or less frequent than those of depressed adolescents. A few years ago, I heard two high school seniors on a train discussing how tearful they often were, even when not feeling sad. One of them said that she distinguished this mood from that of crying when she felt sad, and that her family referred to this special state as "leaking." Leaking may be a result of adjustments to changing hormone levels, increased empathy with others or transitional events. The paired opposite of frequent crying is a state in which a teen doesn't seem to be able to express emotions, appears "flat" and feels empty.

Loss of sexual desire isn't something parents are likely to know about, as this is not a subject most teens discuss with their parents. Indeed, it is something that many teens do not identify on their own, but when asked by a health care practitioner, they will think back and realize that they haven't been masturbating or thinking about sex. Teens who are in a sexual relationship will sometimes say that their partner has been complaining about their lack of interest in sex.

Depressed teens also report that their feelings towards their friends have changed. They are less interested in friends, and less tolerant of their moods and shortcomings. They may describe this as a coldness in their feelings. In general, depressed teens often feel irritable about things that they coped with easily in the past, and they find few things about life satisfying.

John used to drive his parents nuts, spending hours hogging the bathroom, dyeing his hair a rainbow of colors and scouring local thrift stores for cast-offs that fit his idea of style. They were pleased when he returned to his natural hair color and started to dress more conventionally. But when they noticed that he didn't use deodorant regularly and didn't pay careful attention to what he wore, they continued to be concerned.

There are other reasons that John may have changed his

habits so drastically, but a simple style change is an unlikely explanation. If he had just decided to present a more conventional appearance, it is unlikely that he would, at the same time, choose to stop showering or wearing deodorant. If this change was a political or philosophical move, his parents would have heard about it repeatedly. Teens who are upset or sad about something might neglect taking care of themselves for a short period of time, but if this neglect takes place over a long interval it is probably a sign that something else is going on, and depression is a likely cause. John was depressed, and improvements in his personal hygiene were the first signs that he was feeling better.

It Isn't Your Fault

Stan is a severely depressed 14-year-old. He was hospitalized after a suicide attempt one month ago and, despite medication, he still appears to be sad, hopeless and unmotivated. His mother wonders what she did wrong. His doctor says that it is all "chemical," but his mother doesn't believe this.

Many parents are convinced that they are responsible for their children's depression. This isn't surprising as most of us tend to blame ourselves for our kids' problems. We are less likely to take credit for the positives. Parents who don't blame themselves are better able to help their teens. The teen may pick up on the parent's confidence and feel reassured that the depression is no one's fault—not his, not yours.

It is unlikely that there is one cause for depression. Although each researcher tends to focus on a single area, such as genetics, body chemistry, early childhood experience, family issues, and personality, it is likely that there are not only a variety of possible causes for depression, but that in any one person, more than one of these factors is involved.

Researchers are interested in investigating the causes of depression because with more precise knowledge will come new, more effective treatments. Finding specific causes for certain kinds of depression may also lead to accurate laboratory tests to diagnose these kinds of depression.

In Chapter 3, I will deal with the major types of depression and the different ideas about the causes of depression. Many parents want to know "Is this my fault?" They will learn that depression is an illness. It is not caused by someone's bad behavior. Although environmental factors, including those in the family, may have some triggering or contributing role, there are also many other factors that cause depression. You need to move past feelings of guilt and, instead, focus on what you can do to cope with your teen's depression. But before you and your physician decide on a course of treatment, it's important to have a correct diagnosis.

The next chapter will tell you more about adolescent emotions, so that you can gain a better understanding of the developmental changes your teen is experiencing.

2. Adolescent Emotions

Bill has always been quiet and introspective, even when he was a very small boy. Although he says he doesn't feel sad any more often than other teens, he doesn't get excited easily, and he sometimes talks about the sharp contrast he notices between himself and his boisterous, outgoing best friend. He and his parents worry that he is, or will become, depressed, although his parents have always been pleased that he hasn't caused them any trouble.

Bill and his parents are worried about Bill's temperament, which is related to both his mood and his emotions, but not the same thing as either. Although we often talk about feelings, most of us don't really think about what they mean. Having a low-key temperament such as Bill's is not the same thing as having low spirits. It is important to distinguish between the quietness of a long-standing depression and the calm personality traits that may make someone appear low in spirits.

Temperament and Emotion

Temperament is a person's emotional climate, the enduring, overall group of emotions that he or she most commonly feels. A teen's temperament would include whether she is cheerful or serious, optimistic or pessimistic, difficult or easy. Parents may notice clues to their offspring's temperament in the first few weeks of a child's life. Often a child's temperament seems to be similar to that of one of her parents or another family member. Sometimes it seems to be totally foreign. It would be reasonable to assume that temperament has a strong genetic component, but that it might also be influenced by the fetal environment (hormone levels, nutrients, sounds) and experiences in infancy.

If temperament is climate, then mood is the weather. Mood is the predominant emotional state of an individual over a relatively short period of time. Like weather, mood is affected by emotional storms or other brief climatic events. Mood may be determined by the emotions most frequently experienced over the course of a day or two or by experiences that evoke particularly strong feelings.

Emotions, or feelings, are harder to define. Taking place in the short term, they don't always fit with a person's temperament, or even with a person's mood. Philosophers have taken many approaches in an attempt to understand emotion. Some see life without emotion as a black-and-white photograph, with the presence of emotion adding color. Others see emotion as a reaction to exciting stimuli. The French philosopher René Descartes described systems of emotion, and outlined six primary emotions. According to his theory, the primary emotions include joy, sadness, love, hatred, wonder and desire. These basic elements combine to make a myriad of other emotions such as hope, shame, jealousy and greed.

A Time of Change and Growth

Amy is almost 14 and just finishing Grade 8. About once a week
for the past month she has come home saying that she feels very
depressed. The last time, she said, "No one likes me, and I'm
going to fail all my subjects." She ran upstairs and threw herself
on her bed, sobbing. The first time this happened, her mother
tried to talk with her, but Amy just told her to go away. She ate
supper with her family but didn't talk to them. The next morning
she seemed cheerful and back to her usual self. Her good mood
lasted for almost a week, and then her moodiness came back.
Her mother thinks Amy is being manipulative and dramatic and
trying to get attention. Her father says that she's just acting like
a teenager.

A teen at this stage of development tends to see everything in
black and white. An unintended snub from a friend means
that no one likes her and, further, that no one ever will. A
call from a friend means that she is popular and will stay
that way. Parents might think that one episode of misery
after a fight with a friend—which is quickly followed by rec-
onciliation on the phone that night—would be enough to
make their teen realize that the next fight will probably also
be resolved quickly, but they are looking at the situation
from an adult perspective, not from a teen's.

At those times when she was sobbing on her bed, Amy
really felt "depressed," but no parent or doctor would say
that she was suffering from depression. The term *depressed*
means one thing to a doctor and another to the teen. Amy
has felt sad before, but may have expressed it differently. As
a teen, she is learning to observe herself and her feelings in a
way younger children do not, so the sadness takes on additional meaning. On some level, probably not conscious, she

is also throwing herself into the feelings that she's having, as an experiment aimed at answering questions, such as "What does it feel like to be really sad?" and "Do I feel better if I cry?"

As teens grow and mature, we see less of these mood swings. Adolescents learn strategies to moderate their feelings and learn that there are often gray areas between the black and the white.

Development and Depression

In my line of work, adolescent medicine, development is everything. Our knowledge of how children go through the process of becoming adults guides almost everything we do in this field. There is no set timetable for this process. Cognitive and emotional development do not happen in a smooth, predictable fashion, for each teen moves back and forth through the timeline of maturation in her own fashion and at her own pace. Some knowledge of the developmental process will help you understand teen depression, by giving you a "road map." You will be able to see how developmental issues may have contributed to a depression, and how the depression is affecting the teen's normal development. It may also suggest some successful strategies for helping your teen get through a depression.

Depression is a problem that can occur at any age, even in infancy. It can be difficult to diagnose in children. Signals of depression, such as decreased energy in a very energetic child who still has "normal" levels of energy, can be hard to evaluate. However, researchers have fairly convincingly shown that the incidence of depression increases with age. Studies of depressed mood (that is, feeling down, not the same as clinical depression, of course) have shown that about

10 percent of 11-year-olds and about 40 percent of 14-year-olds experience feelings of depression.

Doctors, psychologists and others often talk of "growth and development," but although both result in significant positive change, the processes are quite different, with growth going in only one direction. Growth and physical development are much more predictable than cognitive and emotional development.

Physical Changes

Growth and pubertal development can be stressful for teens as well as for their parents. Teens may feel as though they wake up with a different body almost every day, as hair sprouts, voices change, menstrual periods start and "life-threatening" acne appears. Overwhelming changes in body size and shape, with weight doubling for both males and females between the ages of 10 and 17, can lead to body image problems, a significant source of stress and anxiety.

These rapid changes are a physical metaphor for the many emotional changes of adolescence. Teens cannot ignore the emotional changes of this age because they have obvious physical reminders that life will never be the same.

Worries about puberty add to this stress, with many teens feeling that their physical growth or the outward signs of their sexual maturation are unusually early or late. Someone who is teased about his adolescent development may experience lowered self-esteem and depressed mood.

As adolescence progresses, however, teens usually accept the changes in their bodies. Attempts to change are no longer aimed at covering up or enhancing puberty, but at fitting into a cultural norm of what is attractive.

Concrete and Abstract Thinking

Some of the biggest changes in adolescence are cognitive, that is, related to thinking. Teens develop increased sophistication in their thought processes throughout adolescence. In childhood and early adolescence children are "concrete thinkers." Like Amy (see page 19), they see things in black and white. For the most part, they are unable to take a general concept and deduce a specific rule or idea from it. They also have difficulty developing a general idea based on a specific idea or experience. As adolescence progresses, the teen's ability to think more abstractly develops, often first in areas least associated with his personal life. Parents may not see any evidence of this sophistication, but teachers may notice it in essays and class discussions. Later, these thinking skills become evident in a personal and social context.

One hallmark of concrete thinkers is that they tend to think in extremes, and are convinced that whatever they are experiencing in the moment is their permanent state. For example, a young teen who has had a fight with her best friend may believe that no one likes her and that no one ever will. A concrete thinker who is depressed might be even less able than other depressed people to see that his feelings and life situation might improve.

Some kinds of therapy may work better for teens who can think more abstractly. Also, a teen who is depressed may find that her cognitive abilities are blunted, so that even though she has developed abstract thinking skills, she seems to be unable to use them, and is thinking much more concretely. This can lead to academic and social difficulties for the teen.

Autonomy

Achieving personal independence, or autonomy, is a key task of adolescence in Western cultures. It is intertwined with a sense of mastery over one's environment, an ability to accomplish some basic day-to-day tasks, an acceptance of growing up and a feeling of personal security.

The quest for autonomy starts long before adolescence. Throughout childhood, the child acquires the skills and knowledge needed for the healthy development of autonomy in adolescence. In early adolescence, the young teen begins to express autonomy by showing a decreased interest in participating in family activities and by mood swings. These rapid changes in mood are real but are exaggerated by the teen's need to be separate from parents.

It can be difficult for a parent to determine whether a seemingly isolated and unhappy teen is depressed or working through autonomy issues. One distinguishing feature is that a teen who is functioning well, socially and academically, but who has mood swings at home is less likely to be depressed.

Young teens may practice autonomy through their fantasy life. When imagining themselves more grown up and able to navigate complex situations, they might fantasize about suicide or dying. In my experience, many teens have imagined killing themselves even though they're not actually feeling suicidal, that is, they have no desire to die.

Teens may explore and express their autonomy in risk taking. Frequently, these activities involve risk to family relationships (such as when family rules are broken) rather than risk to self. When a teen begins taking major risks, such as drinking and driving, having unprotected sex or dropping out of school, it can be a sign of unhappiness, depression or even suicidality.

As teens express the need for autonomy, parents sometimes pull back, either out of exasperation or because they want to give the teen room to grow. This space is important, but autonomy cannot develop well if the teen feels abandoned. He needs to feel secure to effectively move away from his family. A depressed teen may become more depressed if he feels he is not getting any attention or that his parents don't care about him.

Physical development, the drive for autonomy and increased self-awareness are all factors in increased privacy needs. This can, again, make it more difficult to ascertain a teen's moods, feelings and thoughts. Teens need to feel that their thoughts are private, and parents may feel they are walking a tightrope between respecting this need and determining whether a teen is depressed or suicidal.

Friendships

Teens' friendships are an important bridge from dependence on parents to reliance on self. Friends can listen more dispassionately, give opinions that would not be heard if they came from parents and participate in the shared experience of growing up. Teens pay attention to their friends' behavior as a measuring stick or mirror. A friend's positive approach to adversity may give an adolescent ideas about how to deal with her own stress, but a negative approach can also influence her.

In early adolescence, a teenager's mood often seems linked to a relationship with a best friend. It is not that the friend is "making" him feel the way he does, but rather that the feelings are a reaction to the ups and downs of the relationship.

After a while, friendships broaden and include not only

more people, but often a wider variety. Peer activity is more group focused, and identity with various groups is expressed through clothing and hairstyles. A teen who feels she doesn't fit in with a group identity because of issues of race, class, poverty, illness or other unfairness can feel isolated.

Identity

Another important task for the teen is the development of a sense of identity. Children have an identity from a very early age, but are not particularly aware of it. Trying out different modes of being, including ways of speaking, dressing, acting and thinking, are ways of discovering whether an identity fits.

The search for identity can be a process of extremes. Teens often start with behaviors or beliefs that are the opposite of their parents'. When parents see actions or categorical statements as judgments on their own deeply held beliefs, they may find it hard to be supportive of the teen who is in need.

Development of a conscience is part of this process. A young person may feel guilty about past actions. If he is depressed already, that guilt can feed into the situation. Young people may also feel guilty about their increasing sexual feelings and the struggles they may have incorporating sexual identity into their overall self-identity. Sexual dreams, fantasies, wet dreams and masturbation can all be sources of anxiety and feelings of guilt. The adolescent who is feeling attracted to teens of the same sex may also feel confused and isolated.

Competence and Self-Understanding

To adequately achieve the developmental tasks of adolescence, a teen must have a reasonable level of competence. Competence is the ability to use resources, both internal and external, to achieve a goal. Varying resources are available to teens. Internal resources may include temperament, intellectual skills and interpersonal skills; external ones may include supportive adults (parents or others), educational opportunities and friends.

One might assume that more resources would make a teen more competent, but this is not always the case. Previous experiences of competence at earlier developmental tasks, secure feelings of attachment to parents in early life and a perception that one can control some aspects of one's life are more important than volume of outside activities. Depression hinders competence. It is hard to utilize resources when you lack concentration and energy, and when nothing seems enjoyable. We could also speculate that lack of competence might make someone feel more depressed.

Self-understanding is another part of adolescent development that plays a role in depression. Young children define themselves in terms of their bodies, their possessions and what they can do in fairly absolute terms. As they develop, they start to see themselves more in terms of what they think and how they feel, comparing themselves to their perceptions of others. They start to understand their own competence. All of these factors contribute to self-understanding. If a teen develops a self-understanding that includes perceptions that he is helpless but also responsible for negative events that happen to him, he may be more likely to become depressed. Depression can also cause a distorted self-understanding, as it will include perceptions of being a guilty, hopeless person.

Emotional Awareness

Somewhat related to self-understanding is emotional awareness. Teens interpret their emotions and perhaps even feel them in a different way than younger children. They learn to monitor their emotions and to express them in more sophisticated ways. Parents often see some experimentation with this expression as overly dramatic behavior. A teen who expresses sadness may do so in a way that is more understated, and it may go less noticed. Statements about suicide could be misinterpreted as histrionic.

The Resilience Factor

Jules is a 14-year-old who has just moved into a group home for teens. He has been in four foster homes in the previous five years. He was taken from his mother, who was depressed and alcoholic, when he was nine. His father left when Jules was three, having physically abused him for more than a year. Jules has changed schools twice mid-year since being taken away from his mother. In spite of this he does well in school and has managed to maintain some close friendships. He was the only Grade 9 student this year to make the soccer team. Although Jules sometimes talks about feeling sad about his situation and about missing his mother, he shows no signs of depression.

Jules would seem to be at high risk for depression, but he is obviously very resilient. An interesting and relatively new field of medical research is the study of resilience, that is, how some people stay healthy in the presence of risk factors.

Some protective factors exist within the teen. Temperament is clearly one of them. Some people seem to be born optimistic and with a huge capacity for happiness. Being able to do things well (like Jules's soccer abilities) also seems to be protective, so the teen who makes friends easily, achieves well in school or attains other skills is less likely to become depressed.

For some teens (though not Jules) there are also factors within the family that promote mental health. Teens from families that are close but not overbearing and who feel supported by their parents are less likely to become depressed. Clear boundaries such as rules that are fair but that delineate appropriate behavior are also protective.

There are also protective factors outside of the home. Teens who feel there is someone they can talk to and who feel respected by an individual outside of the immediate family are less likely to be depressed. Jules may have had a teacher or child protection worker who filled this role.

How Can You Help Protect Your Kids?

Many risk factors for depression are unchangeable. As we have seen, girls are slightly more prone to depression than boys. However, you, as a parent, may be able to mitigate some of the things that might lead to depression in a girl by examining your expectations of your daughter. Maybe you are unconsciously promoting some old-fashioned, stereotypical views of how women should behave and can change your attitudes or expectations.

Many adolescents who (like Jules) would seem to have the deck stacked against them do quite well in life. In the past, we have often asked what makes some children vulnerable to social and other factors, but nowadays we are wondering what makes them resilient—that is, what gives some teens the ability to resist high levels of stress and have a positive outcome. Like gender, some of the factors that promote resilience cannot be changed. Temperament is one of these. Teens who are optimistic, autonomous and who easily develop good social skills are at a definite advantage. A genetic predisposition to good mental health would be another.

The fit between parents and children is also important. Many teens do well because their parents are able to respond to their particular temperament or difficulties. There are also situations in which the parents' natural parenting techniques can cause friction, despite their good intentions. The fit between parents and children is something that cannot be easily changed, although parents can learn new tactics to deal with a teen who is not responding to the approach they have been using (perhaps one that was successful with the teen's brother or sister).

A parent who is mentally healthy and resilient is more likely to have a child who shares these characteristics. This is probably the result of a combined genetic and parenting effect, with the parent modeling positive responses to stress. It may be that treating parental depression and other mental health problems can make children more resilient. Children are then in a healthier environment and have a model that tells them that it is possible to change and grow.

You now have a better understanding of your teen's emotions and the risk—and resilience—factors for depression. The next chapter will explain the different types of depression and outline some of the possible causes.

3. The Many Types of Depression

As a parent, you don't actually have to figure out what kind of depression your teen has, or what is causing it. Your job is to find someone who can diagnose your teen and find her appropriate help. (Turn to Chapters 4, 5 and 6, which deal with available treatments, if you want to know right now what you can do.) However, there are several kinds of major depressive disorders, and understanding where your teen fits in the spectrum may help you to anticipate what could happen and make decisions about treatment. This chapter describes the major subtypes and outlines some theories about the causes of depression.

Types of Depression

When a depression first starts, it can be difficult to determine its type. There are several different kinds, some of which are somewhat controversial. We can't assume that because it has gotten worse over the winter it is seasonal affective disorder (SAD), for instance, and it can take a discerning practitioner to distinguish between substance abuse and some forms of depression.

Major Depressive Disorder (unipolar depression)

Major depression, sometimes called clinical depression, is characterized by deep despair or an extremely depressed mood, lasts two weeks or more, and includes at least four of the following symptoms: sleep problems, appetite problems, lack of energy or interest, feelings of worthlessness, hopelessness and/or guilt, difficulty concentrating, irritability or suicidal thoughts or attempts. All of these except irritability are also criteria for adult major depression.

About 50 percent of people who experience a major depression will have at least one more episode at some time in their life.

Some of the types of depression described below (SAD, postpartum depression and psychotic depression) are subtypes of major depression.

Normal Depressed Mood

Thirteen-year-old Sandra came home from school looking upset. She went up to her room and was still lying on her bed two hours later when her mother went up to tell her that supper was ready. When Sandra's mother asked Sandra how she was feeling, the teen said, "Don't bug me," and added that she wasn't hungry. The next morning Sandra looked tired but got to school on time. After school she came home with a friend and they listened to music. Sandra ate supper with the family and seemed fine.

It is important to remember that people have many reasons to feel down or blue. The length of time it takes to feel better depends on the reason for the mood, the personality and temperament of the teen, and the availability of support systems. Parents don't need to worry unless the teen starts to display signs of a major depression, or unless the depression seems out of proportion to the severity of the loss (compared to other teens, not to you or other adults) or unless there seems to be no triggering event. Sandra was experiencing a normal depressed mood, not a clinical depression.

Adjustment Disorder with Depressed Mood

Leo's family moved to a new neighborhood. He still attended the same school, but instead of living next door to his best friend, he was now a 15-minute walk away from him. Everyone else in the family felt pretty settled in after a month, but Leo felt disorganized and out of place. He seemed to be very irritable and started mercilessly teasing his younger sister, with whom he had always enjoyed a good relationship. He wandered around the new neighborhood aimlessly. His teachers complained that he wasn't paying attention in class.

Because adolescence is a time of development and change, troubles in adjustment are common. They also can be associated with depression. Teens with such troubles do not meet the criteria for a major depression, although a major depression could develop. A diagnosis of major depression would not be made unless the symptoms persisted for a couple of months or unless there were major problems, such as suicidal thinking. This diagnosis is made if the reaction to the new situation is disproportionate to the event (either in strength or duration) and has a negative impact on the teen's ability to function either socially or at school.

Secondary Depression

This is a depression that happens as a result of another illness, either psychiatric or medical. These are discussed in more detail in Chapter 9.

Dysthymia

Susie has had the same group of friends since Grade 5. She is now in high school and she hangs out with them after school. Her nickname for the last year has been Eeyore, because she seems to be gloomy and negative all the time. She starts most statements with an apology, such as "Well, this is probably stupid, but ..." Susie and her friends have almost forgotten that she was once involved in a number of activities, liked to dance and laugh and was considered fun to be around. Some of the kids wonder why they are friends with her, but she has been part of the crowd for a long time. Her parents think it's funny that she has turned out to be their "quiet one," but she does okay at school and has friends, so they aren't really worried about her.

Dysthymia (pronounced dis-THI-me-uh) is sometimes referred to as mild depression, but this designation does not recognize the serious effect it can have on a teen's life. This type of depression was originally named and described by Hippocrates and means "ill-humored." Unlike normal depressed mood, it is a chronic problem. People with dysthymia manage to go to school or work, but they tend to be the "Eeyore" of the crowd—gloomy, and with low energy. Their mood is depressed and they tend to have low self-esteem and some symptoms of major depression (appetite change, sleep problems and low energy), but in a milder form. Compared to major depression, there are fewer physical symptoms but more emotional symptoms such as gloomy thoughts and anhedonia. These young people, often worriers, are unable to see the humor in situations and are somewhat passive and self-deprecating.

Although there may be a precipitating event, dysthymia often creeps up on a teen. She may blame herself for not being able to "snap out of it." After a while, a person with dysthymia forgets what it was like to feel happy or content, and her depressed mood starts to feel like a normal state of functioning. In some ways this dragged-out feeling can be more debilitating than a major depression that lasts for a shorter period of time.

Dysthymia can be found in teens who abuse substances, those with eating disorders and those with anxiety disorders (they can co-exist), and it can have a large impact on a teen's life. Teens with this type of depression tend to have difficulties at school and problems with friends and relationships. They get sick more often than their peers. They don't seem to notice good things that happen to them and tend to overreact to negative things.

A diagnosis is made if the teen has been depressed throughout most days over the course of a year. They must also have two of the classic symptoms of depression, as outlined in Chapter 1. Girls are twice as likely as boys to develop dysthymia. It tends to have its onset in adulthood, but does occur in children and teens.

Seasonal Affective Disorder

A number of people feel psychologically well in the spring and summer and start to feel depressed in the fall. By winter this feeling has turned into a full-blown depression that includes low energy, excessive fatigue, increased sleep, increased appetite with a craving for carbohydrates (such as candy, bread and potatoes) and weight gain. A diagnosis of seasonal affective disorder (SAD) is not made until two or three episodes have occurred.

As with almost everything else, SAD has been more thoroughly studied in adults than in teens, but one good-sized study in Washington, D.C., showed an overall rate of possible SAD in 3.35 percent of teens studied. The rate was lower for younger students and highest for girls who had finished puberty. This is the same type of pattern seen for depression in general, with rates escalating during puberty.

The farther north you go, the more likely you are to find people who suffer from SAD. In Canada, up to 5 percent of people have this problem. Interestingly, one exception to this seems to be Iceland, where a recent study showed almost no SAD (no one knows why this is).

Seasonal affective disorder (*affect* refers to mood) seems to be caused by a lack of light. Light has an effect on brain hormones and possibly on neurotransmitters (chemicals that transmit messages between the brain and other nerve cells). Scientists have not been able to determine exactly how the message regarding light exposure gets to the brain, but until recently it was assumed that this message traveled through the eyes, with a visual image of light carried through the optic nerve. However, new research seems to suggest that the message may actually be carried through the bloodstream, with light triggering something in the blood cells that are in vessels that run close to the skin. Blood vessels in the eye don't have any skin covering them, so the eye would be an important part of this system, but not necessarily the only part. Light therapy is used as treatment (see Chapter 6).

Summer depression also occurs. It appears to be more common the closer one gets to the equator. The symptoms are almost opposite to those of winter depression—insomnia, poor appetite and weight loss. High summer temperature is a possible cause.

Bipolar Disorder

Also known as manic depression, bipolar disorder has a strong genetic component. It involves alternating cycles of very high highs and very low lows. Some teens can start with a depression that looks like a major depression and develop the mania later. The episodes tend to begin suddenly and escalate quickly. Although the majority of people with this disorder get it in their early twenties, it can start in the teen years. About 1 percent of adults have bipolar disorder.

Diagnosis in an adolescent requires at least one manic episode. Teens with major depression who have a family member with bipolar disorder are more likely to develop bipolar disorder than depressed teens with no family history. Manic episodes often start with the teen feeling energized, self-confident and talkative. He is fun to be around and may draw other teens into risk-taking behaviors. He is oblivious to any problems his inappropriate behavior may cause. If the mania increases, he develops poor judgment and his previously fun behavior goes over the edge. Friends feel embarrassed by the things he does, but he doesn't notice. He may become hostile, agitated and hyperactive. He talks more and more, with his ideas racing from one unrelated thought to the next. He has grandiose ideas and feels he can do anything. He may become more sexually active without thinking of the consequences of his actions for himself or others. He may spend huge amounts of money, using savings or parents' credit cards. He is likely to ring up large long-distance and 900-number bills. He sleeps less while seeming to have more and more energy. Some-times he may even have delusions and hallucinations. These attacks can last two or three months.

The earlier, less florid stage, called hypomania, may persist instead of moving on to the extremes. Hypomania seems to be associated with increased creativity, and artists with bipolar disorder may be reluctant to be treated for fear of losing this creativity. Crying jags are common in teenagers with hypomania.

The depression stages may last longer than the mania, but in between, the teen may feel perfectly normal; and he may miss the feelings he had when he was manic.

Mania shares features with attention deficit hyperactivity disorder—impulsivity, hyperactivity and distractibility. However, ADHD is a lifelong problem and will not have a sudden onset in adolescence. Moreover, it may be difficult to distinguish a first episode of mania from the onset of schizophrenia, as both can involve paranoid delusions, hallucinations and grandiose ideas. Schizophrenics tend to have a wider range of delusions and much more disordered thought processes than people suffering from mania.

Bipolar disorder can also be confused with anxiety disorders or conduct disorder. However, the teen with conduct disorder tends to be hurtful to other people with a vindictive motive. The manic teen may also be hurtful, but more by not realizing or denying the consequences of his actions.

Hyperthyroidism with its jitteriness, increased appetite and difficulty sleeping can also be mistaken for mania.

Substance abuse, especially of stimulants such as speed, can lead to a state much like mania. The cycling between the "manic" and the "depressed" states is often much more rapid than in bipolar disorder.

Bipolar disorder can have a huge impact on the life and development of a teen. In addition to all the consequences of depression, manic episodes are often associated with substance abuse, self-harm, school failure and criminal acts. In the long term, development is affected, as mania disrupts the teen's ability to form and maintain relationships and interferes with the process of learning to regulate emotions as well as the other tasks of maturation.

A subtype of bipolar depression is *cyclothymic disorder*, with frequent alterations of hypomania and depression, occurring over at least two years.

Although bipolar disorder is usually treated with drugs, psychotherapy can help too, in a number of ways. If a teen can reduce the number of stressful events that occur and learn stress management techniques to deal with inevitable stressors, the illness may recur less often. Both depressive and manic episodes can be destructive of interpersonal relationships; a therapist can help the teen find ways to rebuild them. Sleep deprivation can provoke manic episodes, but with the help of a therapist the teen can organize his life with an emphasis on routines and avoidance of activities that lead to decreased sleep, such as substance abuse. Untreated bipolar disorder carries a high mortality rate from suicide and injuries.

Postpartum Depression

Postpartum "blues," directly related to hormonal changes, occur in at least 50 percent of new mothers. While we don't tend to think of postpartum depression as a teen problem, many young women have children while they are still only adolescents themselves. The symptoms—depressed mood, tiredness, poor concentration, sleep problems and anxiety— are usually short-lived. About 7 to 10 percent of new mothers experience more persistent and severe symptoms, which generally appear by the time the baby is a month old or after the cessation of breast-feeding. Irritability and mood swings often occur, in addition to the symptoms noted below.

In some teens an ongoing feeling of hopelessness and depression may develop. Whether this is also related to hormonal changes is less clear. A young mother may have many reasons to feel sad or hopeless. She has had a sudden change in life role. She is now responsible, often on her own, for another person's well-being. She may be feeling insecure about her ability to produce enough breast milk. She is probably sleep deprived. She may be coping with poverty for the first time. If she is living on her own, she may have realized that she lacks some basic skills, such as cooking, banking or knowing how to shop for food. She may be getting messages from family members, acquaintances and even strangers that she is not old enough to be a good parent.

Of much greater concern than postpartum depression is postpartum psychosis, which carries a real risk that the mother will kill her child. In this condition, severe postpartum depression is accompanied by hallucinations and delusions. This is rare, with less than 0.5 percent of new mothers developing the condition.

Premenstrual Depression

Premenstrual syndrome (PMS) is a group of problems that occur in the second half of the menstrual cycle. Symptoms include feelings of depression, irritability and lethargy. Increased sleep and overeating are also commonly cited as being part of PMS. Researchers have been considering shifting the sleep patterns, including missing a night's sleep, as a treatment for those who suffer from PMS.

Psychotic Depression

People who meet the criteria for a major depressive disorder and who also have delusions or hallucinations, and who are not diagnosed with schizophrenia or a similar disorder, are considered to be suffering from a psychotic depression. Teens are more likely than adults to experience auditory hallucinations with a depression. And teens with these symptoms are more likely to go on to develop bipolar disorder than those with a depression not involving these symptoms.

They are usually treated with a combination of antidepressant and antipsychotic medications. (See Chapter 4 for more about medications to treat depression.)

Theories about the Causes of Depression

Although there are many different theories about the development of depression, they are not mutually exclusive. It is likely that in any given depressed teen, there is an interaction between genetic, physiological and psychological factors that predispose the individual to a depressed state.

Stress

One factor that might tip a predisposed teen into depression is stress. Some level of stress is positive, as it motivates and stimulates: stress can lead to the development of new coping skills and it can advance maturity. At high levels, however, it can be paralyzing or, when biologic risk exists, plunge a teen into depression. Events that seem equally stressful may have different effects on different people, some events leading to depression, others to anxiety or grief. In different teens, what seem to be equal stressors may have a large effect on some and much less on others.

Shame

Researchers and other professionals in different psychological fields have looked at the role of shame in depression. Although this is often a much more striking aspect of adult depression, adolescents with depression also identify feelings of shame. Guilt and shame are intertwined feelings, with guilt involving self-blame and a sense of fault, and shame leaning more towards embarrassment, humiliation and disgrace. Guilt is about personal actions or omissions, whereas shame is stimulated by a wider variety of things happening within the self.

Shame can arise from a number of experiences. Many parents use shaming as a parenting tool, trying to get their children to behave by encouraging them to feel bad about themselves. The classroom is another environment where shame is frequently elicited.

Children may be more susceptible to the negative effects of shaming if they have a personality or temperament that is more passive, or patterns of thinking that involve a spiral into helplessness.

Psychoanalytic Theories

Psychoanalytic theories assume that there are both conscious and unconscious aspects to the mind. For example, Sigmund Freud believed that infants and children move through stages defined by body parts—oral, anal and phallic phases. Difficulties at any of these stages could cause what he called fixation points that would be reflected in the personality of the child. Fantasies and wishes are pushed into the unconscious (repressed) if they are in some way unacceptable to the individual. Freud saw depression (or melancholia) as a tortured grief involving the loss of the "introjected love object" (the mother, whom the baby ingests through breast-feeding) or as ambivalent feelings towards someone else, turned against oneself. The difference between grief and depression in the Freudian system is that with grief the world feels empty, whereas with depression the person feels empty. Freud did, however, wonder if there might be a biological basis for some depressions.

Other Psychodynamic Approaches

Like psychoanalytic theory, psychodynamic theory holds that internal conflicts arising in early childhood are at the root of depression. These conflicts are diametrically opposed feelings, such as a need for dependence and a desire for independence. The internal, unconscious struggle between these feelings becomes evident as depression, although the teen is unaware of the basic conflict. Conflicts can also exist because of differences between the reality or perception of self and the ego ideal (what one aspires to be). Childhood experiences that damage self-esteem, as well as losses and disappointments in early life, are also seen as contributors.

Behavioral Theory

Behavioral theory postulates that there are external stimuli that we respond to, resulting in an outcome, and that we learn from these interactions to respond in certain ways to certain groups of stimuli. The outcomes are reinforcers (negative or positive) of our responses. Early behavioral analysis of depression saw it as a decrease in response to stimuli, therefore reducing reinforcers for the behavior. Such a decrease in response might be precipitated by a loss (of a goal or relationship) that would reduce reinforcers, and a ripple effect would spread the results to other situations. A person might also be lacking in the social or interpersonal skills needed to evoke reinforcement. They might also be unable to perceive reinforcers because of anxiety.

Another behavioral theory is that of *learned helplessness*. In this model, a child learns that she cannot influence the outcome of any situation. As an adult she assumes that she is helpless, and cannot control her destiny. This theory also involves the idea of attribution. When people fail or succeed, they tend to attribute the outcome to either external or internal factors. People who attribute success to external factors and failure to internal factors are frequently more prone to depression. (In other psychological models, this is known as internal or external locus of control.)

Cognitive Theory

Cognitive theory deals with thoughts. It is based on the idea that each of us has an individual construct of the world. Units of thought are used to figure out new information and experience. Thought always comes between experience and emotional response. Problems in information processing, such as overgeneralizing or drawing conclusions from poor data or from the wrong set of data, can lead to a pattern of continuing errors. Depression might then be seen as a process joining emotion, thought and action in a negative way.

Aaron Beck, the originator of much of this work, proposed that there were three cognitive aspects of depression: negative views of oneself, of the world and of the future. Negative thoughts and experiences are magnified and positive ones minimized. A stressful experience, or one that triggers a memory of a negative childhood experience, can precipitate a move into the more negative cognitive pattern, and depression ensues. This negative pattern would exclude any ability to buffer oneself from common feelings of depression—sadness, hopelessness and shame.

Interpersonal Theory

Interpersonal theory suggests that people with depression are overly dependent on relations with others. This could be for a variety of reasons, including poor family relations in child-hood. Factors such as family violence, growing up with a depressed or substance-abusing parent and childhood neglect can all play a role, as they tend to be related to inadequate affectional bonds. When a teen who has been raised in these conditions experiences a loss, she becomes depressed. In addition, her problems with interpersonal relations can make her feel depressed. Conversely, intimacy and high-quality social bonds are seen as being protective against depression.

Parenting Theories

I am not a big believer in blaming parents for all their children's woes, although there is evidence that the extreme of bad parenting is related to depression. Harsh punishment of children (such as shaming, referred to above) has been shown to increase their risk of becoming depressed either in childhood and adolescence or in adulthood. Childhood physical and sexual abuse are strongly linked to adult depression and suicide. Moreover, if the early loss of a parent through death or family breakdown leads to long-term family problems such as child neglect, it is associated with depression later in life.

Most studies of parenting and depression examine levels of "attachment" (the bonding relationship) between parents and children. It is thought that poor attachment can result in a child seeing first his parents and then all other people as unhelpful, not responsive to his needs and even rejecting. Also, poor attachment in early life might continue as a parenting style that is unsupportive and that does not protect against stressful events both within and outside the family.

Biological Theories

The idea of evil "humors" that arise both within and outside the body, thus affecting the soul, is an old one and more biological than psychological. More recent evidence that physiological factors are involved with depression includes findings that depressed teens can have abnormal cortisol (an adrenal hormone), growth hormone and thyroid stimulating hormone responses. Older depressed teens also have what is called shortened REM latency—that is, a shorter period of sleep before rapid eye movement sleep.

Neurotransmitters

Biological theories being researched today tend to focus on neurotransmitters (the action of many antidepressant medications is based on the function of neurotransmitters). These are chemicals that are used to pass messages between the brain and other nerve cells. The places where this communication occurs are called synapses. An impulse moves from a presynaptic cell through the synapse to a postsynaptic cell. Receptors on cells respond to these chemicals and either activate or suppress electrical activity. Scientists describe the specific receptors as being like locks on the surfaces of cells. Neurotransmitters are the keys that fit into these locks, starting a sequence of chemical and electrical events in the cell, just as the key to your car starts the ignition. There are many neurotransmitters and also chemicals that mop up excess neurotransmitters. Monoamine oxidase inhibitors, some of the first effective antidepressant medications, work by decreasing the levels of an enzyme, thus increasing the availability of some neurotransmitters.

The belief that physiology plays a part in depression is supported by the apparent genetics of depression. Although a "depression" gene has not been identified, bipolar illness shows a strong family predisposition, even in cases where siblings or twins have been raised apart. Offspring of depressed parents show a higher lifetime risk of both substance abuse and major depression than people who were not raised by depressed parents. There is some evidence that the risk of depression is higher if it is the mother who was depressed and that the age of onset in the parent correlates with the age of onset in the child. However, since these studies were done in families where the children were raised by their parents, it is difficult to separate the apparent inheritance of depression from family environment factors. One such factor is parental unpredictability. When feeling well, a parent might be able to appropriately praise or discipline a child, but when under stress the same parent might not be able to respond to positive behavior. A parent's anxiety or depression might also have negative effects on his relationship with the other parent, and the ensuing discord might increase risk of depression in the child.

It is clear that stress can change levels of neurotransmitters. If there is an inborn vulnerability in some people to depression, then perhaps what this means is that less stress is required to change the levels of neurotransmitters. There are probably levels of stress high enough to cause at least a short-term depression in anyone.

Interest in neurotransmitters has focused recently on *serotonin*. Many studies have shown that in depression the levels of brain serotonin are reduced, and there are changes in the receptors for it. Serotonin transporters are important proteins, as they help move serotonin from the synapse, when it has delivered its chemical message, back to the presynaptic nerve, as part of a serotonin recycling program. If the level of brain serotonin is reduced, this would have two effects. In the short term, it would increase serotonin effect, as it would sit around the synapse instead of being taken back to the presynaptic cell. In the long term, the serotonin would degrade without being reused, resulting in a serotonin deficit where it was needed. A gene predisposing to depression could be turned on by stress or other events. This might decrease serotonin transporter protein synthesis, leading to decreased availability of serotonin. Newer medications that act on serotonin uptake have further supported the role of serotonin in depression. (See Chapter 4 for more about medications.)

Other neurotransmitters may also be involved. Over the years there has been interest in norepinephrine, a hormone related to stress that is also a neurotransmitter. Absolute levels have been investigated, as well as the balance between the hormones norepinephrine and acetylcholine. Acetylcholine may be involved in biorhythm disturbances, leading to sleep disorders and perhaps to worsening of depression.

Quite a few studies have looked at the role of neurotransmitters in suicide. When brain tissue from adults who have committed suicide was examined, decreases in serotonin-binding sites were found in one part of the nerve and increases were found in others, compared with brain tissue of people who have died of other causes. These changes have been most pronounced in areas of the brain that involve inhibition and disinhibition. Decreases in serotonin effect in these areas could increase impulsivity. These changes are not just seen in the brains of depressed people who have killed themselves, but in those with other psychiatric disorders as well. Researchers were surprised a number of years ago when a couple of studies showed that men taking drugs to lower cholesterol levels were more likely to die of suicide than those who weren't taking such drugs. In animals, low levels of cholesterol are associated with decreased serotonergic function, so there may be a link between the two.

NEUROHORMONES

Neurohormones, such as adrenocorticotropic hormone (ACTH), made by the pituitary gland or its controlling hormone, and corticotropin-releasing hormone (CRH), may also be involved in depression. These hormones control levels of cortisol, which is made by the adrenal glands. People who are depressed have lower cortisol levels and less daily variation in these levels than people who aren't depressed. Other neurohormones, such as growth hormone, may be involved in some of the physical symptoms of depression.

Certainly, the common wisdom of the day is that "raging hormones" are related to many adolescent behaviors and feelings. It is unlikely that this is the whole story, as increased levels of depression in the teen years correlate better with age than with the stage of puberty that a teen has reached. Hormonal changes could influence the emergence of depression in a number of ways.

Hormone levels in adolescence are no higher than those of adulthood, but the levels can increase from prepubertal levels abruptly and can fluctuate radically. These fluctuations could have a direct physical effect on teens, making them more excitable and vulnerable to sudden mood changes by altering neurotransmitter or endorphin (morphine-like hormones made by our bodies) levels.

Teens may react to the changes in their bodies (pubic and underarm hair, acne, breast or penis development) with a variety of feelings—guilt, pleasure, increased self-consciousness, lowered self-esteem—some of which might feed into feelings of sadness. Many of the psychological theories mentioned above regard loss and grief as important experiences in the development of depression. Some teens seem to mourn the loss of their childish bodies, potentially precipitating a depression. Teens who develop early may feel burdened by increased expectations placed on them by peers, parents and teachers.

Infectious Disease Theory

In the mid-1980s, papers started to appear postulating that Borna disease virus (a virus that causes brain infections in horses and sheep) might be associated with human mental illnesses, especially cyclic depression. An early study showed that almost 2 percent of a group of mentally ill patients had antibody to the virus, whereas none of the control group did. When groups of patients with unipolar and bipolar depression were compared with healthy controls, the rates were more than twice that. Since then a number of studies using a more sensitive test—the Western Blot—have shown even higher rates of exposure in depressed adults. There is some evidence that the problems are caused not by the virus itself but by the immune system's response to the virus. It is not clear how this virus would be transmitted to humans from animals. No antiviral treatments are currently available for Borna disease virus in humans.

Now that you are familiar with the different kinds of depressive disorders and with a number of theories about the causes of depression, you are in a better position to make a decision about how to treat your teen. The next three chapters discuss a variety of treatments for depression.

4. Medications in the Treatment of Depression

Families often find it hard to sort out the information they get about depression treatments. It comes from a huge variety of sources—the Internet, television, newspaper articles, friends, doctors and therapists. Some of this information comes from people who want to convince you that the treatment they are proposing is the best. Someone who has extensive training in one type of treatment will feel validated if you pick this type. A friend might feel reassured that she made the right choice if your teen has the same treatment as her son or daughter. And, of course, there are people who are primarily interested in selling you their particular services, whether they are appropriate or not. With any treatment, you must ask yourself, "Is there any evidence that this works?"

Finding this evidence may be difficult, but it is important because you waste time and money trying ineffective treatments. Meanwhile, your teen may feel unhappy, hopeless and perhaps even suicidal. Moreover, some treatments haven't been tested, and others have been researched in a less than satisfactory manner. You also need to consider that much depression research has been done with adults and is not always generalizable to teenagers.

Although it can be very helpful to talk with someone who

has had a treatment you are considering, this person's insight is not the same as evidence. Evidence, to be valid, must be based on large numbers of people who have used the treatment in controlled conditions. These results should then be compared with a control group—people who thought they were getting the treatment but weren't.

Your doctor may have up-to-date advice, but you should expect any practitioner to tell you why she is recommending a particular treatment, what you can expect from it (both positive and negative effects), how long it might take to work, how much it costs and how she will monitor your teen's progress. She should react to questions in a nondefensive way. You should view with suspicion broad statements, such as "This always works," or, "There are never any side effects." Everything has possible side effects. We often think that unwanted effects are associated only with prescribed medication, but they can also occur with herbal therapy, psychotherapy and alternative treatments.

Treatment Is Essential

In the face of warnings about side effects, delays in positive outcomes, expense and lack of evidence for many treatments, you may be tempted to do nothing and see if time will heal the depression. Although this can happen, it isn't guaranteed, and no one wants to watch a teen suffer emotionally, academically and socially while worrying that he will kill himself. Depression can be treated and it should be treated.

Treatment of depression should always start with an assessment by a medical doctor—family physician (or general practitioner), pediatrician, psychiatrist or internist. The doctor will make sure that there is no other illness causing the problem. Only medical doctors can prescribe medications for depression. Other practitioners who provide counseling or therapy for depression may have doctoral degrees in psychology, social work or education, but they are not medical doctors, even though they are addressed as "doctor." (See Chapter 5 for a detailed discussion of types of therapists.)

Are Drugs Really Necessary?

Once a diagnosis of depression is made, your doctor will probably prescribe a course of medication. The history of psychiatry, and the misuse of psychiatric treatments to silence those who question authority in some countries, makes some of us feel uncomfortable about treating depression with medication. We do not want teens to be "doped up" or turned into "zombies." However, it is becoming clear that depression and other psychiatric illness are caused by chemical disturbances or imbalances in the brain, and it makes sense that medications are going to be the best treatment for these conditions.

Of course, medications must not be used unnecessarily. Many feel that drugs are overprescribed, and that we as a society are overdependent on medication. Parents are often reluctant to allow their teenage children to begin drug treatment —and they have a point. Increasingly, we seem to see "taking something" as the answer to all of life's problems. Small amounts of pain are instantly treated with anti-inflammatory agents, a fever must always be brought down (despite evidence that a fever helps us fight infection), colds are treated with antibiotics (even though they are caused by viruses that do not respond to these medications) and mood variations deserve at least a cup of herbal tea, if not a prescription for an antidepressant.

It's not surprising, then, that many children and teens come to believe that the main solutions to problems are pharmaceutical. A teen may shrug off responsibility for his moods and feelings, seeing them as something a doctor can easily fix by prescribing the right drug, rather than something in which he is an active participant. Because of this trend to see life as a treatable condition, normal extremes of emotions are sometimes misinterpreted as pathological. A teen may start to view herself as diseased rather than as a normal person who is feeling bad. On top of this, adolescence itself is often regarded as a disease by parents, teachers and the media.

Another reason to fear an overuse of medication for depression is that health insurance plans and HMOs are looking for ways to cut costs, and it is much less expensive to give someone a prescription than to pay for psychotherapy. This mindset encourages quick treatments that are standardized and not labor intensive.

Sometimes Antidepressants Are the Best Approach

For all the reasons discussed above, some people believe that teens should not be treated for depression with medication. While their response is understandable, a blanket no-drugs policy is not a wise approach.

There is a place for medication in the treatment of depression, after careful assessment and in conjunction with psychotherapy or supportive counseling. The trick is to make sure that the teen really does have a major depressive disorder before treating him with drugs. I recommend antidepressants for the majority of patients who fit the criteria for a major depression and whose lives are affected by the depression in a significant way. About 25 percent of the time they can be prescribed on the first visit. However, a longer assessment that includes tracking a daily mood rating on a calendar that they bring to each session (see page 56) is warranted for many patients. I do not prescribe antidepressants unless I feel reasonably sure that another physical or mental illness is not the cause of the patient's problem.

Even if psychotherapy is recommended as well, antidepressants can help. Psychotherapy is a long process, and a depressed teen who would like to feel better quickly can become discouraged. Antidepressants can help the teen stick with psychotherapy, while she begins to feel better enough to feel hopeful. Moreover, some teens are so depressed that they cannot motivate themselves, or be motivated by others, to participate meaningfully in psychotherapy. Their depression may be so great that it immobilizes them. A teen in this state may feel so hopeless that he cannot believe anything could help, and he may not be willing to try anything that takes an effort on his part. In these cases, antidepressants are used early in the treatment to relieve the immobilizing effects of the depression and bring the teen to a level where he can be an active participant in his treatment.

Doctors may seem quick to embrace pharmacological treatments because they have been trained to make it a priority to try to cure diseases and to make people feel better. Even types of psychotherapy that have been proven effective may make people feel worse in the short term while they are dealing with painful feelings and life experiences. We may be hesitant to make people feel worse even if, in the long run, they will know more about themselves and learn skills to fight their depression.

Before Medication Is Started

Fran is a 17-year-old whose parents insisted that she go to their family doctor after she had spent several weeks moping around, sleeping poorly and not eating. Before this, she had been very active, but in the past six weeks she had stopped seeing many of her friends and even seemed to be looking for excuses not to see her boyfriend, asking her parents to tell him she had a headache when he called and telling him that she was grounded for staying out late. The family doctor spent about 20 minutes talking with Fran and felt that she met the criteria for a major depression, with her low mood, statements like "nothing can help me feel better," weight loss, difficulties falling asleep and frequent crying episodes. He started her on an antidepressant to be taken about an hour before bedtime.

Fran noticed an improvement in her sleep within a few days of starting the medication. She felt more rested in the morning and found herself more able to concentrate at school. However, she was still crying often and still seemed to be avoiding social situations, particularly with her boyfriend. Finally, after coming home from a date with him, in tears and with a black eye, Fran told her mother that he was harassing her with jealousy, put-downs and finally physical abuse. But he always apologized and said he would kill himself if she left him. The family doctor had not asked Fran any questions about her relationship with her boyfriend or other friends. If he had, he would have realized that her depression had a specific situational cause and was probably not a major depressive disorder at all.

A full assessment of the teen by a physician should include questions that lead to a picture of how the teen is feeling not just on that day, but over a longer period of time. It should include questions about sleep, appetite, mood, sexual orientation, suicidal feelings, the teen's idea of why she is experiencing her current mood, her level of hopelessness and physical symptoms. There should be questions about relationships with friends, family members, boy/girlfriends, teachers and peers. The doctor should ask about previous episodes of depression, mania or psychosis. Even if there are no indications of a physical problem, a physical examination should be done, unless another physician or nurse practitioner has done one recently.

The doctor may want to order some blood tests, but there should be a specific reason for doing so. A "shotgun" approach, where a number of tests are ordered to screen for problems, is not warranted. Similarly, regular blood tests are not required while patients are on the most commonly used antidepressants, although they may be required for other classes of medications.

I find it helpful for the teen to rate her days on a one-to-ten scale, with one being extremely suicidal and ten being the best she has ever felt. I ask her to mark her calendar with a rating every night and to bring it back the next week. This gives me a better idea of how the teen is feeling than her recollection would. It is helpful to continue this practice as treatment progresses. Frequently, teens will say that they aren't feeling any better, but when we look at their chart, they have gone from twos and threes to fives and sixes without noticing.

Some doctors use a standardized test to gauge the patient's level of depression. Teens tend to like filling out these forms and may admit on them to feelings that they wouldn't tell a doctor about right away. Also, these questionnaires can be repeated every couple of months to measure the progress that has been made.

General Information about Medications

As discussed in the last chapter, the chemicals used to pass messages between brain cells, as well as between other nerve cells, are called neurotransmitters. There are a number of different neurotransmitters. The contact between neuro-transmitters and brain cells starts a sequence of chemical and electrical events in the cell. Chemicals called enzymes mop up neurotransmitters outside the cells. This regulates levels of neurotransmitters outside the cells, preventing excess accumulation. It is thought that imbalances in neurotransmitter levels are associated with depression. Most antidepressant medications are known to have an effect on neurotransmitters.

The Placebo Effect

When evaluating the usefulness of a drug, the placebo effect must be taken into account. Patients given pills that actually contain no active ingredient often feel better than those who receive nothing, apparently because they expect to get better. (I remember reading a study from the 1970s of a painkiller in which the placebo worked better than the drug.) It is important that patients and investigators not be able to figure out which patients are taking the medication that's being tested and which are taking the placebo. Patients also report a wide range of side effects when taking placebo pills. This is true not just of treatments for psychological problems, but also for physical ailments.

Good studies of medication effects always involve a control group of patients who get an inactive medication that looks, smells and tastes the same as the active medication. However, this can be difficult to achieve if there is a frequent side effect or a taste that is hard to replicate.

A recent meta-analysis (where the results of a number of studies are put together to try to get more valid results) suggested that success in treating depression with drugs could sometimes be attributed to the sense of hopefulness conveyed by the doctors and their belief that the drugs would work.

Side Effects

All medications have side effects (the effects of a drug that do not help the problem being treated). Some drugs have a number of effects that may be useful in different situations, so the "side effect" of drowsiness in an antihistamine used for allergies is the desired effect when it is used to aid sleep.

Side effects are not always negative. Side effects of the birth control pill, for instance, include control of acne and decreased menstrual bleeding, which protects against anemia. Obviously, we don't worry about positive side effects.

It is important to remember that not every negative physical symptom experienced while taking a medication is a result of the drug. People get headaches, diarrhea, constipation, rashes and other problems even when they are not taking medication. In addition, when on a medication we may expect side effects, and even exaggerate them out of worry. Because we are on the lookout, we may be aware of things going on in our bodies that we might not normally notice.

Your teen's doctor should explain the common side effects of a medication and what to do if he experiences one or more of them. The doctor should also explain serious, rare side effects. Doctors who don't have weekend and night coverage (usually a group of doctors share this responsibility) should not be prescribing medications, in my opinion. However, a doctor who has a small practice and prescribes drugs that have few or only minor side effects may be able to get away with a message on her answering machine instructing the caller to go to an emergency room if there is a problem with a medication.

Many teens, especially girls, will not take a medicine if they think it will make them gain weight. Even if weight gain is a rare side effect, it could still affect the teen's decision to start or continue a medication. It is important to ask about its effect on weight when the drug is prescribed.

The prescribing doctor should be told about any other medications your teen is taking. Because serious drug interactions can occur, tell your child to disclose any medications or drugs, whether they are prescribed, over-the-counter or illicit. If she seems reluctant to provide this information, make sure she knows that the doctor-patient relationship is one-on-one, and that you won't be told anything she doesn't want you to know. For example, she may not want to tell the doctor about being on the birth control pill, worrying that you will find out.

Find out what would happen if your teen took more of the drug than is prescribed, even as much as a whole bottle full. Some medications that are fairly safe on their own can be lethal if an overdose is combined with other medications.

Don't Expect Instant Results

Although medications to reduce fever or take away pain usually work within 45 minutes, antidepressants are different. Because the changes take place over three to eight weeks, they can be quite subtle, so keeping a chart, as discussed above, can help show their effect and assure you or your teen that the medications are doing their job. Try not to run out of medication, as stopping abruptly can cause problems.

The doctor should give instructions about what to do if a dose is missed.

Some antidepressants have a sedative effect and are prescribed to be taken before bedtime. Others have a stimulant effect and are prescribed to be taken in the morning. If the instructions on the medication label just say "Take once a day," ask the doctor for the correct timing.

You can ask the doctor to write down both the brand name and trade name of the drug, its possible side effects, what to do if a side effect occurs, or if your teen misses a dose or loses her medication while the doctor is away. Don't be embarrassed about asking to have all this written down—it can be hard to remember all the information.

In the majority of cases, the first drug prescribed is effective, but there is no way for a doctor to tell in advance whether a certain drug will work for any particular adolescent. It is not an error in judgment if medications have to be switched; it's just a matter of finding the right prescription for your child.

The doctor should be able to give you some idea of how long it will be before you see a positive effect. Many medications are started in low doses that can be increased every two to three weeks as needed. Although the doctor should not be promising a miracle cure, he should be presenting the treatment in a way that encourages hope and promotes a feeling that the teen and the doctor are a team working together.

None of the antidepressant drugs listed in this chapter are addictive. Once your teen has reached a dosage that works, it is unlikely the medication will have to be changed, unless she grows significantly, which could increase requirements.

Stopping Antidepressants

Most teens who take medications stay on them for at least six months. You and your teen can talk to your doctor at the six-month mark to discuss stopping the medication, especially if the teen has been feeling totally well for three months or so.

When it's time for your teen to stop taking the medication, be guided by your doctor. Antidepressants should not be stopped abruptly. If medication is abruptly stopped, the teen can experience withdrawal symptoms such as nausea, diarrhea, restlessness, tremors, sleep problems and nightmares. The doctor should give your teen a schedule to taper the dose over at least several weeks. It can take several months to come off SSRIs (selective serotonin re-uptake inhibitors) completely. While the teen is tapering off medication, it is a good idea for him to start keeping a daily mood calendar again. If the depression seems to be returning, the dose should be increased to its former level.

Some teens take antidepressants for much longer periods. This may be because the depression has improved but there are still some symptoms of depression, or because a major change is anticipated that might trigger a relapse (a move, change of schools or impending parental divorce, for instance). Drugs will also be continued longer if she has a history of attempting suicide or if there has been a need for more than one medication at the same time.

Selective Serotonin Re-uptake Inhibitors (SSRIs)

You will know your teen has been prescribed an SSRI if the prescription is for fluoxetine (Prozac), fluvoxamine (Luvox), citatopram (Celexa), sertraline (Zoloft) or paroxetine hydrochloride (Paxil)—these are the most commonly used SSRIs. Venalafaxine is an SNRI (see below).

These new antidepressants have changed the face of depression treatment because they are effective, have side effects that tend to wear off quickly and overdoses are usually not lethal. Clinical trials of some SSRIs have shown them to be effective in more than 50 percent of teens taking them.

SSRIs are classed together because they have the same effect, reducing the breakdown of the neurotransmitter serotonin by decreasing its delivery to the chemicals that mop it up. This action increases the amount of serotonin in contact with cells and, in a way that isn't totally understood, these increased levels lead to improvement in depression.

Unlike some other classes of drugs, SSRIs are not always similar to each other chemically, so switching between them to reduce side effects or increase efficacy can be a useful move. Often lumped in with this group are the serotonin-norepinephrine re-uptake inhibitors (SNRIs), which have not yet been adequately tested on teens.

One of the biggest advantages of this group of drugs is that it is difficult to overdose on them. Anyone with a depression serious enough to be treated with medication is at increased risk of committing suicide, so the potential lethality of the medication is an important consideration. A number of studies have shown an increase in suicidal thinking and suicide attempts in early treatment of depression no matter what course of treatment is chosen: SSRIs, other antidepressants or psychotherapy. Whether or not your teen is on antidepressants, it is important to take him to an emergency room if he is suicidal.

Another big advantage of SSRIs is that they need only be taken once a day. It can be hard for anyone to remember to take medications, and depression makes it even harder. Patients tell me they find it much easier to remember a once-a-day medication.

Many teens experience at least one side effect during the first month of SSRI use, but most of these effects disappear on their own as the body adapts to higher levels of serotonin. Because there are serotonin receptors throughout the body that are affected by these drugs, side effects can occur in most body systems. Side effects should be reported to the prescribing doctor. Common side effects include nausea, sleepiness or insomnia (depending on the medication), itchy rash, muscle aches, nervousness, sweating, dry mouth and appetite problems. Rarer side effects include visual problems, chest pain, vomiting and menstrual problems. Adverse effects can often be avoided by starting with a low dose and slowly increasing to an optimal dose.

A rare side effect called frontal lobe amotivational syndrome has recently been described in both adults and teens. Teens who experience this side effect feel unmotivated; they also have memory problems and feelings of being separated or distant from other people. This syndrome can be hard to diagnose as a side effect, as the symptoms are also signs of depression. Lowering the dose often results in improvement.

There have been seemingly contradictory reports about weight loss and gain on SSRIs. Early in treatment, teens may experience nausea and even vomiting, with an accompanying loss of appetite. Also, some teens experience an increase in appetite or food intake as part of a depression. As the depression lifts, their eating may slow down, leading to weight loss. Later on in the treatment, some people gain weight when they are on SSRIs. This weight gain may be a long-term effect of increased serotonin levels on receptors in the brain's appetite control center.

Teens who are thought to have unipolar depression may actually have a bipolar disorder; they have simply not experienced a manic episode yet. In these cases, SSRIs treat the depression but can also trigger a manic or hypomanic episode. This happens in less than 0.5 percent of patients who start on SSRIs.

Jane was a budding poet when she became depressed at age 16. At first, her depression gave her lots to write about, but as her depression worsened, she became unable to write. She had great hopes for positive results from the SSRI that I started her on and her depression improved dramatically after about three weeks. However, she was still unable to write, not for any lack

*of inspiration or ideas, but because she couldn't find the words
she needed.*

Memory problems are being reported more and more often
in people using these drugs. One of the most common experiences is difficulty finding words. People either lose words
altogether or substitute one that sounds similar even though
it has a different meaning. Other memory difficulties have
also been recognized. University students on SSRIs have
had serious academic problems as a result of short-term
memory loss. They notice that they can no longer count on
cramming a large amount of material the night before an
exam. A simple remedy to overcome memory problems is to
change antidepressants.

Most teens will not tell their parents if sexual dysfunction is one of the side effects they are experiencing—indeed,
while they are depressed they might not even be aware of
the problem. But as a teen begins to feel better, it is normal
for him to re-engage in masturbation or a sexual relationship. It can be disturbing for a teen to find him- or herself
slow to arouse and/or lubricate, having "blah" orgasms or
being unable to achieve orgasm at all. It is unclear how
often sexual dysfunction on SSRIs occurs. Doctors may feel
uncomfortable asking patients about this aspect of their
lives, or may worry about being accused of sexual miscon-
duct if they do ask. An easy way around this is for doctors
to give patients an information sheet listing possible side
effects of the medication with a note asking them to report
any they experience. Teens with sexual problems on these
medications are often switched to buproprion (see below).

There was a worry that at least one SSRI might promote
tumor growth. However, large studies have not been able to
show this effect and, in fact, have shown a decreased incidence
of one kind of tumor in lab animals and slowed growth of

one human cancer cell line in the lab. It is considered safe to give these drugs to people who have cancer.

SSRIs should not be taken with monoamine oxidase inhibitors (MAOIs) as serious reactions have been found when at least one of the SSRIs, sertraline, was given with an MAOI. Patients became confused, agitated, delirious and even comatose, and also experienced major changes in heart rate and blood pressure. SSRIs should probably not be combined with sedatives, alcohol, some antihistamines, erythromycin, cisapride or ketoconazole.

Because SSRIs are metabolized in the liver, you should tell the prescribing doctor about any history of liver disease, such as hepatitis. If the teen has no ongoing liver problems, it is probably fine to take SSRIs, but the doctor will probably want to take blood to check liver function before prescribing them.

As mentioned earlier, SSRIs should not be suddenly withdrawn; use should be tapered off. A study of SSRI users with learning disorders and depression showed that 40 percent had symptoms of withdrawal when they stopped taking paroxetine, while none experienced withdrawal problems with fluoxetine. Other studies have shown withdrawal symptoms with all the SSRIs. Babies born to mothers who are on SSRIs are also at risk for withdrawal and should be monitored, as there is speculation that they could have seizures or feeding problems. The pediatrician might even consider giving the baby small amounts of the drug and tapering it off over a couple of weeks. Good antidepressant choices for a pregnant teen who plans to nurse are sertraline and paroxetine, which are secreted into breast milk only in small amounts.

Buproprion

Buproprion is not usually used as a first line of treatment for adolescents because it hasn't been tested on teens as thoroughly as some other drugs. However, because it has been shown to be useful in treating attention deficit hyperactivity disorder, it may be the first drug tried for a teen with ADHD and depression.

In addition to being an antidepressant, buproprion has also been shown to decrease craving for nicotine in adults. It would be reasonable to try this drug in a teen who smokes cigarettes and is also depressed.

The action of this drug is not known. It has no effect on monoamine oxidase and much less effect on serotonin than the SSRIs. It has an effect on dopamine, a different neurotransmitter.

The biggest problem with buproprion is that in high doses (above 400 mg/day) it has been associated with seizures. The risk is highest for people who have had seizures before or who have eating disorders, so it should not be used with either of these groups. This drug should not be given with other medications that increase the risk of seizures. People taking buproprion should avoid alcohol, as the combination of alcohol and the drug may also increase the chance of seizures.

Buproprion has not been shown to cause sexual dysfunction, and it is often used in people who have had sexual problems while taking SSRIs.

Weight loss is a common side effect of this drug. Other fairly common side effects are dry mouth, headache, constipation, restlessness, difficulty sleeping or anxiety, especially early in treatment.

Monoamine Oxidase Inhibitors (MAOIs)

Monoamine oxidase inhibitors (MAO inhibitors) were early pharmaceuticals used to combat depression. There is no evidence that they are useful to teens; they are only rarely used for this age group. In order to avoid dangerous side effects, people taking these drugs must avoid consuming chocolate, some cheeses and red wines. This is another reason not to use them in adolescents, given the amount of discipline and attention to detail needed to avoid these foods.

MAOIs can interact with some asthma medications, narcotics, SSRIs, cough medicines containing dextromethorphan, insulin and illegal drugs such as narcotics, cocaine and amphetamines.

A newer group of MAO inhibitors, called reversible inhibitors of MAO-A (RIMAs) has been developed. Food restrictions are not necessary when taking these drugs, and they are not toxic to the liver. Moclobimide, the most widely tested RIMA, has been shown to be as effective as tricyclics (see below) for both unipolar and bipolar depression in adults, but it has not been well tested on adolescents. Some doctors feel that this drug is useful in depressed teens with attention deficit disorder or social phobia (see Chapter 8 for more information).

Tricyclic Antidepressants

These drugs have been found to be ineffective in teens, although they are useful in the treatment of adult depression. I discuss them mainly because some teens are prescribed them in low dosages for bedwetting and, if a depression develops, the doctor might want to try an increased dosage to see if there is an antidepressant effect before adding in another medication. Your doctor may have some other specific reason to try them on your teen, so ask about this if tricyclics are prescribed. Like SSRIs, tricyclics seem to prevent the re-uptake of both serotonin and norepinephrine and possibly other neurotransmitters.

In common with many drugs, tricyclics can have side effects. It is important that teens on these drugs use strong sunscreen (number 25 or 30) and stay covered up, as tricyclics cause sun sensitivity. Serious side effects that have been reported include muscle problems, seizures and breathing problems. More common, less serious side effects include dry mouth, a bad taste in the mouth, a drop in blood pressure upon standing (resulting in dizziness when rising quickly), drowsiness, constipation, urinary problems and blurred vision. Some of the tricyclics can cause sleepiness.

Tricyclics can interact with a number of drugs, including alcohol, sedatives, cimetidine, quinidine, procainamide, dicumarol, disulfiram and oral contraceptives—any of which may be taken by teens.

An overdose of tricyclics can be fatal. As teens with depression are at higher risk of suicide than other teens, this is a major concern. Tricyclic antidepressants should be prescribed only in small amounts.

Your teen has been prescribed a tricyclic drug if any of these names is on the prescription label: imipramine, desipramine, nortriptyline, amitriptyline and doxepin.

Lithium

Lithium is an element that is found in nature as a compound, usually lithium carbonate or lithium oxide. It is an electrolyte, like sodium and potassium. Just after World War II, John Cade, an Australian psychiatrist, discovered the sedative properties of lithium in animals and started treating manic patients with it. It was approved for psychiatric use in the United States in 1969.

Lithium is most often used for bipolar disorder and is also sometimes used for recurrent major depression. It is still a very useful drug for people with bipolar disorder. The majority of those who use it experience either resolution of their symptoms or episodes that are less frequent, shorter or less severe. For people who don't respond to it, using lithium with another medication often helps. Lithium is noted for stabilizing extreme mood shifts without causing a tranquilized feeling. Teens are less likely to be successfully treated with lithium than adults, although we don't know why this is so.

Like other antidepressants, lithium affects neurotransmitter activity, but scientists are only beginning to understand how it works. Unlike other antidepressants, which seem to have an absolute effect on certain neurotransmitters (for instance, SSRIs always make serotonin levels rise, even in someone with normal levels), lithium has been shown to bring levels of glutamate (an excitatory neurotransmitter) into the normal range when tested on mice. In a mouse whose levels are already normal, there is no effect on glutamate. It is probable that the same mechanism is at work in people, which explains lithium's seemingly paradoxical action in preventing both mania and depression. It has also been postulated that lithium's effect on the distribution of body electrolytes may change the movement of electrical impulses along nerve cells.

Lithium is not a quick fix. It can take as long as a month before significant improvement is seen. As a long-term therapy it prevents or reduces recurrence, but it is not a cure.

The most common and bothersome side effects of lithium are memory and concentration problems, which can be corrected by taking a lower dose—under the prescribing doctor's guidance, of course. It can also cause tremors, thirst, nausea, increased urination and lethargy.

Your doctor should check blood levels of lithium regularly, as it can have toxic side effects if levels are too high. These blood levels should be taken 12 hours after the last dose. The difference between levels that work (therapeutic levels) and those that cause toxicity are fairly small. Signs of a dangerously high level include vomiting and diarrhea, weight loss, extreme thirst, muscle twitching, slurred speech, blurred vision, memory problems, dizziness and irregular heartbeat.

Patients on lithium over the long term can develop hypothyroidism or other endocrine problems and kidney problems, so regular checkups are important, especially as hypothyroidism and depression can cause similar symptoms.

Lithium should not be taken by people who have kidney problems, as the kidneys eliminate lithium from the body, and if the kidneys aren't working, levels could get too high. This excretion is linked to sodium (salt) excretion, so people on lithium should not be on low-salt diets, which could cause sodium levels to fall dangerously low. Diuretics (water pills) should not be taken with lithium. Diuretics are not commonly used in adolescence, but teens with heart problems who often have to take them should not be on lithium.

Lithium should not be taken during the first trimester of pregnancy or by breast-feeding mothers.

One of the most important uses of lithium is to prevent or decrease the intensity and severity of episodes of mania or depression. The longer the patient takes lithium, the better he will get, but once he stops the medication, the beneficial effect ends. Teens often find it a chore to continue on a long-term medication once they are feeling better. They may dislike taking a pill because it reminds them that they are different. They may also miss the highs that go with the manic phase. Or they may just forget to take the pill.

It is important to encourage teens on lithium to take their medication and see their doctor regularly. You or he should call the physician if he experiences diarrhea, vomiting or problems with urination while on the medication. At regular visits, the doctor should ask about any other medication use and check lithium blood levels. Remind the teen that when these tests are ordered, he should follow the instructions and go to the lab at the time specified. It is not safe to be on lithium without accurate monitoring of blood levels.

Anticonvulsants

Two antiseizure medications, carbamazepine and valproic acid (valproate), have been used for a number of years in people with a bipolar disorder that does not respond to lithium. Common side effects are nausea, drowsiness, dizziness and blurred vision. Very rarely, carbamazepine use has caused a serious blood disorder, aplastic anemia. Carbamazepine affects liver enzymes and can therefore interfere with a number of medications. Alcohol should be avoided when taking either of these drugs.

A newer, chemically unrelated, expensive anticonvulsant, topiramate, is also being used for bipolar disorder, but it has not undergone large, controlled trials. A number of reports have suggested that it is useful when carbamazepine and valproate have failed, and it has fewer side effects. These reports are primarily of adult use. Side effects include sleepiness, dizziness, nausea, tremors and problems with vision and speech. It has been used with lithium and MAOIs with no reported problems. Drug interactions have been reported with other anticonvulsants. Because many anticonvulsants that are metabolized in the liver lead to increased metabolism of the birth control pill, unplanned pregnancies can result from combining these two medications, so a back-up contraceptive method should be used. As with other antidepressants, it can take a month or two before a positive effect is noticed.

Bipolar disorder that has not responded to other medications has also been treated with mexiletene, a drug that is mainly used to treat heartbeat irregularities, but also has anticonvulsant properties. In a short, non-blinded (this means that the patients and doctors knew what was being used in each subject) trial of mexiletene in 19 adults, in which the drug was added to other medications, over half of the 16 patients who completed the study showed at least some response.

The decision to use antidepressants is one that parents take very seriously. However, in most cases (other than with bipolar disorder) antidepressants are used for less than a year and often result in significant improvements.

If your teen needs medication, it does not mean that she is weak. She is in need of help, though, and medication can be an important part of that help. As part of a treatment plan that includes counseling or therapy, these drugs can help stabilize the situation and potentially prevent suicide deaths. The next chapter will tell you more about how therapy works, types of therapists and how to find the right counseling for your teen.

5. Psychotherapy for Depression

Sandy was 13 when he was diagnosed with depression. He didn't want to see "a shrink" and seemed angry that his parents and his doctor thought he was "crazy." After some negotiation, his doctor persuaded him to go to a teen group at the adolescent clinic of a local hospital. Sandy soon found the group helpful for a number of reasons. He didn't want to be the focus of a therapist's (or any other adult's) attention. In the group he was sometimes the center of attention but not all the time. He liked a couple of the other boys in the group and felt that if they thought it was okay to go and talk about feelings, then it was probably okay. These boys liked him, too, and this boosted his self-esteem. He had felt very isolated before joining the group and was now able to meet people who had similar feelings to his. He would sometimes make a suggestion to one of the boys and then realize it was something he could try, too.

Parents, too, may think that psychotherapy is only for "crazy" people or that a person who needs help from a therapist or psychiatrist must be "weak." Like Sandy, they may be surprised to find how helpful psychotherapy can be.

Many physicians will recommend psychotherapy as a major part of your teen's depression treatment, either on its own or along with medication. Psychotherapy is a discipline with many different schools of thought and practice. Some therapists specialize in a particular group of disorders or one age group. Some evidence suggests that particular types of psychotherapy are especially helpful for depression in teens. Many therapists who work with teens have found that psychotherapy aids teens in coping with a variety of illnesses and problems, not just psychiatric ones.

All therapies are not created equal, however. Only one, cognitive behavior therapy, has been well studied and shown to be effective, at least for mild to moderate depression in teens. Another, interpersonal therapy, can also be helpful to teens, but there is a shortage of studies that compare a group of depressed teens getting this type of therapy to a similar group getting another type. Some of the more common types of psychotherapy are discussed in the appendix. Most types of therapy haven't been researched in teens at all. We, therefore, don't have any established scientific findings on whether they are helpful for depressed teens.

A Good Teen Therapist Is Hard to Find

Many adults find teens to be difficult in their behavior, impossible to understand and/or members of an alien species, and there are plenty of psychotherapists who feel the same way. Although in many cities there seems to be a psychotherapist on every block, it can be frustrating for teens, parents, guidance counselors and others to realize that many of these therapists don't want to work with teens. No matter where you live, it can be difficult to find a psychotherapist who enjoys teens and who does not have a six-month waiting list. You may feel you should take whatever you can get, and sign up with the first therapist who is available to your teen. However, it is important to try to find out if this therapist is going to be a good "fit."

Remember Aisha? She was the depressed 17-year-old discussed at the beginning of Chapter 1. She'd broken up with her boyfriend, and she was spending hours in her room every day. She had crying spells, wasn't eating and seemed uninterested in seeing her friends. After two months, the family doctor recommended therapy. She gave Aisha's parents the names of a few therapists and they started calling around. The first two were not taking patients; the third had a two-month waiting list. The next two didn't treat teens, but the second-to-last one on the list had an opening the following week; and he took both teen and adult patients. In a phone interview with Aisha's parents, the therapist said that he never used medication and that because Aisha's depression was a result of her breakup with her boyfriend, he was sure a couple of months of therapy would do the trick.

Over the next two months, Aisha did not seem to improve. Her parents asked for an appointment and met the therapist in his office, a sunny room containing three chairs and a Persian rug. The therapist told them that Aisha hadn't really started talking yet, that she needed more time to get in touch with her feelings.

Aisha's case illustrates a number of problems that teens and parents can run into. The first was Aisha's seeming unwillingness to get help. In fact, she was unable to get help; she was too depressed to find the energy to do it. Her parents realized that they would have to take the lead, but when they ran into difficulty finding a therapist who would take her, they quickly decided not to be too picky. They accepted the first practitioner who agreed to treat Aisha, without asking very many questions about how he worked or what his philosophy was.

This therapist was not equipped to do anything except talk and listen. Some teens find it easier to express their feelings through art, writing or even play therapy, but this man was unfamiliar with those approaches. He thought that if he saw Aisha for long enough, she would start talking, and he would be able to help her. It's possible that this would have happened eventually, but Aisha had a real need to start feeling better more quickly.

The therapist was clear that, in his view, medication was unnecessary for teens. Although such an attitude can be reassuring for a teen or parent who does not want medication, it was really a sign of rigidity on his part. A therapist who *always* or *never* thinks medication is needed is not showing the flexibility needed to work with a variety of patients. Although every therapist should have a theoretical and philosophical basis for his work, he should also be flexible enough to know that not every teen can be approached or treated in the same way.

As it happened, Aisha was depressed even before she and her boyfriend broke up. Since her sleep patterns always had been somewhat erratic, Aisha's parents hadn't noticed her more recent sleep difficulties. She was out with her boyfriend, Tom, quite a bit, and when she was at home, they saw her as preoccupied. In fact, her depression was a major factor in her problems with Tom, as nothing seemed to be fun for her anymore and Tom had become frustrated with this. The breakup certainly made her feel even more down, and this is when the depression became evident to her parents. Alarmed by her lack of progress, Aisha's parents found another therapist who felt she was clinically depressed. The new therapist discussed this diagnosis with Aisha's family doctor, who started her on antidepressants immediately. She had art materials for patients to use; Aisha found it helpful to work with clay and, as the antidepressants started to lift her mood, it became easier for her to talk about what was happening in her life and her feelings.

How Therapy Works

Therapists use a number of tools in their work. The most important ones are listening and observing. They notice body language, what the teen avoids talking about and if she is always late or early for sessions. Therapists pick up on recurring themes in what teens tell them. They notice how the teen feels about the therapist and even watch their own reactions to the teen. Some therapists use toys, paint, clay, music, diagrams, dance, photographs and stories to aid their work, while others provide excellent therapy to teens without any of these tools. Some therapists work with techniques from more than one school of psychological thought, but there is no such thing as a therapist who is totally conversant with every technique ever invented, and each should have a solid theoretical basis for the work she does. Therapy can be delivered either to individuals or to groups.

Some important types of psychotherapy are *psychodynamic*, *cognitive-behavior*, *behavior-modification* and *supportive*. These therapies, and some less common therapies, are described in the appendix.

There has not been a huge amount of research on what kind of therapy works for teens, although the field of knowledge is growing. Cognitive behavioral therapy has been shown to have benefits in treating depression, and therapy in general has been found to be helpful, but there is less evidence regarding other specific types of therapy.

Most therapies used to treat depression are based on particular psychological models or theories. These theories were described in Chapter 3.

Self-Help

Self-help is not therapy, but people who use it are often looking for the same outcomes as therapy. We have come to associate self-help with books, usually written by people who have a particular perspective and who often feel that their approach will help anyone with a particular problem. More broadly, self-help could include many of the alternative treatments discussed in Chapter 6. Listening to music, establishing an exercise routine, eating a balanced diet or doing yoga are all ways a teen can help himself feel better, often inexpensively.

Many books that would not be classified as self-help are available that might contribute to a teen's or parent's understanding of adolescent issues. Poetry and fiction can be a source of comfort or inspiration, if chosen wisely. The biggest drawback to therapeutic reading is that very depressed people often don't read much, lacking the concentration and energy to do so.

Self-help books are variable, so if you've picked one that seems schmaltzy, preachy or just dumb, keep looking around. Stay away from any that require an unrealistic approach. Similarly, avoid books that imply your teen isn't getting better because she hasn't followed the instructions correctly, or books that ascribe a wide variety of illnesses to one cause. Some self-help books contain quizzes that allow a teen to put herself into a diagnostic or personality category. Sometimes such quizzes are helpful, especially if the teen has enough insight to describe herself and say, "Yes, I'm like that part" and "No, that bit doesn't fit me," instead of feeling that she must match every category in that group.

The advantage of self-help is that a teen who uses it well can feel able to change. She loses some of her hopelessness and feels empowered.

Types of Therapists

Almost anyone can call himself a therapist, and some excellent therapists do not fit into any of the regulated categories listed below. Often, such unregulated therapists have gone through a rigorous training program that offers a diploma but not the title of "doctor" or a university degree. The difficulty with going to a therapist who isn't regulated by a board or college is that if there are problems, you don't really have anyone to complain to. To be licensed or certified in one of the following groups, you have to meet certain standards. I believe that if you find a therapist you like, who seems to be flexible and not wedded to using only one particular and very specific method (such as hypnosis or sand table play), and who seems to have reasonable training, you should consider her seriously, especially if you have a recommendation from a friend.

Family Doctors

Some family physicians have received training in psychotherapy. If your family doctor offers psychotherapy, ask her what extra education she has received. The occasional weekend workshop is not enough training to be a psychotherapist. You may feel comfortable with your own doctor, or you may want your teen to see someone else. One advantage of family doctors is that their services are covered by provincial health plans in Canada and the National Health Service (NHS) in Britain, and many of their services are covered by private insurance and HMOs in the United States. Some family doctors specialize in adolescent medicine and therefore have an interest in and skills relating to teens. Family physicians can also prescribe antidepressants. You may want to make some inquiries first: Are there special times set aside for psychotherapy? Is the doctor usually on time? (You may want to go and sit in the waiting room to see how long people wait.)

Psychiatrists

Psychiatrists are physicians who have extra training in mental and emotional problems. In Canada and Britain, their specialty status is conferred by the Royal College of Physicians and Surgeons; in the United States, it's conferred by the American Board of Psychiatry. Psychiatrists tend to have practices that specialize in certain age groups. Like family doctors, their services are covered by provincial health plans in Canada and may be covered by the NHS in Britain and private insurance and HMOs in the United States. There is huge variation in the types of practices that psychiatrists have. In an area where there are few psychiatrists, they often spend most of their time prescribing medication, following patients who have psychoses and not doing much therapy. In better serviced areas, there will be others who also do therapy. In any setting, but especially in a university hospital, a psychiatrist may focus on a particular psychiatric problem or areas of problems.

Pediatricians

Although most pediatricians do not practice therapy, some specialize in adolescent medicine and may have extra training or experience in psychotherapy. Like family doctors, they are more likely to provide counseling than therapy, but some have more in-depth training. They can prescribe antidepressants. Coverage of their fees is similar to that of psychiatrists, and their specialty certification is through the Royal College of Physicians in Canada and Britain and the American Board of Pediatrics in the United States.

Psychologists

In many countries, people can call themselves psychologists only if they have a Ph.D. in psychology (or sometimes in education). They have trained extensively, with many years of graduate study after university, as well as clinical training. This degree has a heavy emphasis on research. Graduates must take special exams to be able to call themselves psychologists. They are certified by the Canadian, American and British Psychological Associations. Many private health plans cover the services of psychologists. In some countries, a psychology professional degree (Psy.D.) is also offered; this degree is more clinically focused than a Ph.D.

Social Workers

Many people call themselves social workers—welfare workers and child protection officers among them. These people may have one of a number of undergraduate degrees and are not therapists. However, social workers with an M.S.W. (Master of Social Work) or a Ph.D. in social work may be psychotherapists. They will have had both classroom and practical training. A Ph.D. program also has a research component. They are often, but not always, regulated by regional boards or colleges and have to take exams for certification.

Nurse Practitioners

A nurse may have training in psychotherapy and have a private practice or work in a clinic doing therapy. Nurses are licensed by regional bodies, but there is no therapy certification specifically for nurses.

Other Master's Degrees

Universities in different countries offer a variety of graduate degrees in general counseling, or family and child counseling, and psychology. These two-year courses offer a combination of classroom teaching and practice, with a major research paper required. Some master's degree courses in education also involve counseling training.

Pastoral Counselors

Ministers, priests and rabbis are not all trained in counseling or therapy. Some have taken a few courses, others have received graduate degrees. Most often, they provide supportive therapy. A good pastoral counselor will not force religious views on the teen and will make sure the teen understands that she is not depressed because God has forgotten her, or because she has been bad.

Ways of Delivering Therapy

There are two main configurations that therapy can take: individual therapy and group therapy. However, individual and group therapy are not either/or propositions, as teens are sometimes involved in both. First, let's consider individual therapy.

Individual Therapy

I referred 16-year-old Toni to a therapist while starting her on antidepressants. She was a bit reluctant to go to the therapist the first time, but I was interested to learn that over the next year she never missed an appointment and was never late. I saw her regularly to monitor her medication but she didn't want to talk about her therapy, other than to say that she wanted to continue to go. After six months we tapered her off her antidepressant and I stopped seeing her. I ran into her a few years later at a mall and she told me that the therapy had changed her life. Not only had it helped her depression, she said that it had changed how she saw her life and relationships. She felt that she had never really thought about these things before and that therapy had "opened her eyes." She wasn't sure how it had happened—there certainly had been no "moment of truth"—but at the end of the year she was different and happy with the changes.

Although there are many types of therapists and therapy, they all have similarities. Usually the therapist meets with the teen once or twice a week (counseling or supportive therapy may be less frequent) for between 45 minutes and an hour. The therapist may meet with the parents and teen together sometimes, especially at the teen's request.

The meetings may involve activities such as painting, sculpting or playing with models, or they may be focused on talking. Younger teens are more likely to participate in activities, with older teens being more able to talk. Very depressed older teens often find it easier to express themselves nonverbally.

Most therapists will interact by asking questions, pointing out things that seem to be inconsistent or rewording what the teen is saying. They are much less likely to tell a teen what they think the underlying problem or issue is, and instead wait for the teen to have his own insights.

As a teen progresses in her cognitive development, the possibilities for therapy increase. As younger, concrete thinkers, they rely more on play and games, but as abstract thinkers, they can talk things through, consider hypothetical situations, even see things from another person's perspective.

Although there are occasional magical moments in therapy, when a teen has an amazing insight or is able to see something in a totally different light, most therapy is hard work. Neither teens nor their parents should expect the therapist to "cure" them or to produce any kind of quick results.

Some weeks a teen will talk non-stop about non-issues. At other times, he will find nothing to say. Sometimes at the very end of a session he will bring up an important issue. And even when nothing seems to be happening, a relationship is developing between the therapist and the teen. Many therapists believe that how the teen interacts with and feels about the therapist is a reflection of her outside life and how she relates to others.

It can be helpful to a teen just to know that there is someone who will listen to him in a non-judgmental way and pay attention to him on a regular basis. The teen may come to look forward to her meetings with the therapist as a place and time where she feels protected and understood.

It can be hard for parents to see their teen go off to therapy every week and not hear about what is happening. But you need to respect your teen's privacy where therapy is concerned and not push her or the therapist to tell you what they are talking about.

Don't expect your teen to return from therapy feeling better or seeming happy, although this may happen sometimes. He'll often have a lot to think about after the session. Some teens like to plan for a solitary activity after therapy, like going for a walk or a bike ride.

Group Therapy

Group therapy for children and teens is by no means new, having been in use since at least the 1930s. Group therapy is offered by many types of therapists using a range of techniques and approaches.

One of the advantages of group therapy is that it offers depressed teens a chance to interact with other people who are in the same situation. In the group, they get the feeling that they are not alone, that their experience is more universal than they may have previously thought. Another way the group may help is that a teen can almost always find someone in the group that he thinks is worse off than himself, and take some comfort and inspiration from the strengths that person may show. (See Sandy's story on page 73.)

Support from a group of peers may help a teen feel safe to explore her feelings or the root of her problem. She may become more aware of her real feelings when she hears other teens talking about their emotions.

Teens sometimes develop social patterns during their depression that interfere with the maintenance of friendships. The social isolation that results can help perpetuate a depression. In a group they can learn (or relearn) social skills, as they see the effects of their behavior on others and practice new skills in a protected setting. Teens may observe and adopt strategies that have seemed to work for other group members and practice them on their own, discarding the unproductive approaches they have tried before.

Teens can help each other look at their self-perceptions and encourage some reality checking. Feedback about personal strengths is often more believable when it comes from peers than when it comes from an adult.

If a teen is in one-on-one therapy, she will sometimes be invited to go to a group run by her therapist. This can be hard for the teen; she may feel the therapist is "hers" and can resent attention he pays to others in the group. Problems can arise if some of the people go to the group leader individually and some don't. However, the advantage is that the therapist already knows the teens in the group and has presumably put them together based on his knowledge of them. One would hope that this approach would increase the possibility of a successful group.

Your teen will probably have some specific criteria for a group—mixed or single gender, with known or unknown leaders, same or mixed-diagnosis group make-up and possibly the approach taken by the therapists. Skilled group therapists are good at putting together teens who will work well as a group.

Some groups are time-limited, with everyone entering and leaving together. Others run for long periods of time with a flow of teens in and out. Although the first type of group gives a greater sense of cohesiveness and can be better for group building, the longer-running ones may be helpful for depressed teens, so that the group can focus on integrating a couple of new people at a time. Also, depressed teens in groups often want to sit and observe the first few sessions, and it can be awkward if no one talks.

Young adolescents often prefer a same-gendered group,

with at least one of the leaders being of the same gender also. They tend to prefer, and do better in, a group that revolves around activities, although even in these there will be some discussion. With these younger teens the therapist usually takes an active role, directing the activity and maintaining the rules. A good group leader will be very aware of the tendency of kids in this age group to pick out one or two vulnerable group members and target them for taunting and other abuse; the leader will make sure that everyone is safe.

Groups that focus more on discussion are appropriate for older teens, who have more highly developed thinking skills and are better able to sit and talk without doing something. The group leader will help them develop rules for the group, which will always include a rule about confidentiality. These groups more often include both genders. Older teens in a group often start to feel like a family, discussing their shared feelings of sadness, isolation and despair.

The Search for a Therapist

As mentioned earlier in this chapter, therapists who specialize in working with teens are rare, and sometimes just finding a therapist who is willing to take on a teen is a hard job.

Some teens start looking for a therapist on their own, often because they want the therapist to be "all theirs." Although some feel their parents are their best allies, others have tried to talk to their parents and been told they don't have a problem, or that they should "just snap out of it." Many of these teens realize that they have limited knowledge or energy for this search and enlist the aid of someone else. A school guidance counselor might be aware of what resources are available for a teen in this situation. He probably has a list of agencies and therapists who do not charge fees or who have a sliding-rate scale. There may be peer counselors at school who would also know where teens can find a therapist.

A crisis line, especially one for teens, is another possible source of help. Teens don't have to be suicidal to call one of these phone lines. A friend might be able to help, but she will probably start without any knowledge about therapists, so this is a last resort.

Parents who help their teens find therapists, or find one for them, have a number of things to consider. First, remember that therapists come from many types of professional backgrounds, have a variety of philosophies and, of course, are all unique human beings. No matter what the therapy, the therapist herself is crucial. You will want to find someone with whom your teen wll be comfortable, who sees her as an individual and who does not seem overly rigid.

You can start your search by making a list of any attributes that would be critical to you and/or your teen. Some of these important factors might point you to a specific "brand" of therapist, and some will suggest questions to ask individual therapists. You will want to consider such things as the gender of the therapists, whether they see teens after school or on weekends, what they charge and what type of therapy they do.

Often the best place to start the search is in a community- or hospital-based teen clinic. Not all of these clinics have therapists on staff, but they will be able to make recommendations. Family doctors and pediatricians may also have ideas about which therapists to refer you to. Some employee assistance plans offer therapy or referrals for family members. If you feel comfortable asking friends, they may have some experience with a good therapist they can recommend.

If you are lucky enough to get the names of several therapists who sound good, you can make appointments to meet them either for yourself or for your teen (some offices may want the teen to call and book). Let each of them know that you are looking around. Expect to pay for the appointment. Pay attention to how you feel while booking this appointment. Is the person on the phone pleasant? If you left a message, was your call returned within a couple of days?

When you arrive at the therapist's office, check out the waiting room. Is it reasonably comfortable and neat? Can you hear the receptionist talking on the phone? Did the receptionist ask you personal questions in front of other people in the waiting room? Are there pamphlets about subjects that seem appropriate? Are they aimed at teens? Does the therapist seem to be trying to sell something, like a religion, a nutritional supplement or a herbal remedy?

Is the therapist on time? If there is more than a ten-minute wait, did someone apologize and explain the wait?

You (or your teen) will be asking the therapist some questions, and he will be asking you some. The therapist will want to know what the problem is and whether the teen is willing to commit to the therapy and come regularly for a certain number of sessions. He may want to know why you are shopping around.

A teen who goes on her own to find a therapist is likely to be mainly looking for someone she feels she can connect with. She isn't likely to ask detailed questions about the therapist's approach. If you, as a parent, are searching for a therapist, you may want to ask what kind of therapy he does and where he got his training. He should be able to tell you the average duration of treatment for someone with major depression. Just remember that this isn't some kind of a guarantee—everyone is different.

Assessing the Therapist You've Found

At the end of the first session with your teen, the therapist should be able to summarize the issues for your teen and reiterate goals for the therapy.

The therapist will probably discuss confidentiality. If she doesn't, you should ask what her policy is. Basically, the therapist should tell you that she will not disclose any information about the teen to anyone (including you, her parents) without the teen's permission. The exceptions to this include a legal obligation to report physical, sexual or emotional abuse (usually under a certain age, varying between provinces or states) or serious suicidal or homicidal intent. A therapist who promises total confidentiality without exception is misleading you, or is so lacking in knowledge as to be untrustworthy.

If the therapist tells you that she does a special kind of treatment that no one else in your town does, that it will definitely work after a certain amount of time and that she is misunderstood by the establishment (who are constantly trying to discredit her), be very skeptical. This is how quacks talk.

How comfortable a person feels with a therapist is important, but it isn't an absolute indicator of future success. A therapist who never challenges a patient can be comforting but ineffective. On the other hand, if a teen cannot trust a therapist, that isn't going to work either. If you are a teen checking out a therapist, try to be very aware of how you feel with her. If you are a parent, don't assume that your teen will be comfortable with someone just because you are. He needs a chance to check someone out after you have done some prescreening.

The therapist should outline the costs of the therapy, the chances of your insurance covering it and her billing schedule.

She should not offer to lie about the diagnosis in order to get the parents' insurance to pay for it or barter her services for personal favors.

The therapist should be able to offer a regular appointment time and should outline procedures for canceling appointments.

It is not unusual to try out a few people before finding a good fit, but if you are still looking after seeing three or four therapists, you should start to wonder whether you or your teen are overly anxious about the process and unable to commit to a therapist because of this feeling. It may also be that one of you is feeling ambivalent about getting treatment and therefore quick to find reasons why each therapist isn't the right one.

When Therapy Goes Wrong

Ramuna is a 15-year-old whose family doctor suggested that she see a therapist as an adjunct to antidepressant therapy. After the first couple of weeks, Ramuna started quoting Dr. X all the time, which her parents took in stride, remembering all the teachers she had idolized over the years. But they started worrying when this phase didn't seem to be wearing off. One day, when Ramuna said she would be at a friend's, her parents tried to contact her and she wasn't there. With some prodding, Ramuna told them that she had met Dr. X for coffee and that she had been doing so almost every week. She was incensed that her parents thought this was inappropriate and said that it was okay because they always met in public. "His life is very hard," explained Ramuna. "Everyone tells him their problems, but he has no one to talk to about his." Her parents explained that Dr. X could go to a therapist himself, and meeting her outside the office in this way was not an acceptable thing for him to do. They removed a very

*angry Ramuna from therapy and contacted their family doctor
for advice.*

The vast majority of therapists do a good job in a professional manner and do not mistreat or abuse their patients.
The intense nature of the therapeutic relationship can lead to
difficulties if the therapist is not vigilant or if the therapist
has personal problems that interfere with his ability to
conduct therapy appropriately.

One of the hardest things for a parent is to figure out when
things are going badly. A teen who complains that he doesn't
like a therapist, or that nothing is being accomplished, may
really be speaking out of hopelessness and a conviction that
no therapy can help (thus protecting himself against failure).
He may also be complaining because he thinks it isn't cool to
like a therapist, or because he wants to express anger towards
his parents.

Complaints such as these in the first few weeks of therapy can usually be dealt with by encouraging the teen to give
it a try for a certain amount of time, such as another month.
But if he continues to complain, it may mean that there is not
a good fit between the therapist and the patient. In this case,
it may be time to search for a new therapist.

A therapist who tells you that your teen can get better
only by buying a certain product, which is available exclusively from the therapist, is, in my opinion, definitely unethical. Needless to say, a therapist should not try to get you
involved in a sales organization, in a property deal, in loans
or even in his favorite non-profit organization. (Although
I do think it's acceptable to have posters or leaflets in the
waiting room about charitable organizations.)

Boundary Issues

Many problems with therapists (like Ramuna's therapist) involve what we think of as boundary issues. The boundary between therapist and patient should be very clear, but it can become hazy for a number of reasons. Different therapists have different styles and varying ideas of exactly where the line should be drawn.

These problems can arise in a number of ways. The therapist may inappropriately disclose personal things about herself to a patient. Psychoanalysts often feel that it is very important to keep personal information away from patients. Other kinds of therapists may think that if a teen asks a personal question, the therapist may answer it (for instance, wanting to know how old her children are, or whether she liked the university she attended), but will probably not answer anything that would lead the teen to believe that she and the therapist are friends.

A therapist who gives gifts to a patient is also overstepping the boundary, though again, there are exceptions. An item that is being discarded that could be of use (I recently took some puzzles to the hospital for a bored patient), or a general policy that children and teens are given a small present for their birthday might be acceptable. Most therapists will accept a small present from a patient, especially a handmade item, but will usually turn down expensive gifts.

A therapist should not disclose information or thoughts about other patients to your teen. Some therapists will use an example, such as "Once I took care of someone with a similar problem," and this is perfectly acceptable because there is no identifying information and the story may actually be a composite of several patients.

The issue of sexual abuse of patients is at the extreme end of boundary problems. Again, there is a whole range of behavior that can be seen this way. One end of the spectrum is fuzzy. Some people would say that a therapist should never touch a patient, whereas many of us occasionally touch patients on the shoulder or hand, or even put an arm around them. These are not daily occurrences and do not involve sexual feelings. At the other end of the spectrum the boundaries are clear—therapists should never touch patients in a sexual way or have any kind of sexual relationship with them.

When flagrant sexual abuse occurs, it is sometimes an extension of other behaviors discussed above. The therapist may talk to the teen about his own life, moving into a discussion of his marital problems, sometimes getting quite explicit. He then may move into a sexual relationship. A therapist may convince himself that he is in love with the patient and justify his behavior by ending the therapeutic relationship or by convincing himself that he can keep the two things separate. A different type of abuser is one who preys upon patients in a more cold-blooded manner. He may start with "therapeutic" hugging or body contact and then convince the teen that having sex would be good for her. The power that a therapist has in this relationship makes it difficult for the teen to resist.

Any sexual relations between a therapist and patient are unethical and should be reported to the proper authorities. If the therapist is a doctor or psychologist, a state or provincial licensing authority can be informed of this behavior. Other therapists are regulated in a number of ways and some are outside of any formal structure. In these cases, going to the police would be the only option.

Such cases are rare. The majority of therapists are careful to maintain ethical conduct. You have a wide variety of practitioners to choose from, and you and your teen should be able to find someone that both of you can trust.

When Therapy Ends

In my experience, teens are often unable to reach a definite end to a therapeutic relationship. Adults often come to a mutual decision with a therapist about when to finish, but teens are more likely just to drift off. They start missing or canceling appointments, still come occasionally and then start booking appointments less frequently, eventually stopping altogether. Different therapists deal with this situation in various ways, either telling the teen that if she misses a certain number of appointments she can't rebook, talking about it with the teen and scheduling more widely spaced appointments, letting the teen know that maybe this means she doesn't need to come anymore, or just seeing what happens. If your teen is seeing a therapist whom you have to pay, expect to pay for missed sessions.

The end of therapy can be difficult. Even if it is a mutual decision to end, the teen may feel abandoned or rejected. It can be hard to give up almost an hour of someone's undivided attention every week. The therapist may book an appointment for a month or two later, so the teen can "check in."

Separation from the therapist may echo a teen's gradual separation from his parents and can evoke many emotions. Although good therapists are careful to avoid promoting dependency in their clients, this can still happen and, when it does, it will make separation more difficult.

If the therapeutic relationship has been good, feelings of attachment will have developed, and your teen will miss the therapist and the relationship just as she would miss anyone important to her. Except under unusual circumstances, therapy will not end abruptly, and the teen will have had a chance to discuss his feelings about this important transition with his therapist. He may not need any support from you, but if he does, the best thing to do is to make yourself available for discussion or non-verbal help, maybe by offering to go for bike rides or walks.

Whether psychotherapy works for you and your teen depends very much on establishing an empathetic relationship between your teen and the therapist. If neither psychotherapy nor prescription drugs appeal to you as a way of coping with your depressed teen, the following chapter outlines a number of alternative treatments.

6. Alternative Treatments

Many treatments are available for depression that are neither psychotherapy nor prescription drugs, and some of these are well within the range of conventional treatment. Others are not often used by mainstream doctors. Many people have the idea that all "alternative" therapies are based on herbal remedies such as St. John's wort or ginkgo biloba—but, in fact, some alternatives have been adopted by conventional medicine and some have not. This chapter reviews both conventional and unconventional alternatives.

Before trying any treatment, conventional or not, it is important to rule out any medical problems. You should research an alternative treatment at least as thoroughly as you would research a conventional treatment. Remember that a physician would not treat your teen without his consent; nor should you.

Herbal Medicines in General

Because most herbal treatments are not regulated by federal agencies, you should beware of a number of things. Herbal remedies do not always contain what their labels say they do. If the plants are not cultivated, but are harvested in the wild, gatherers might pick other plants that have a similar appearance or are easier to harvest. Even if the right plants are used to make the remedy, they may be low in the active ingredient because of variables such as soil conditions, water, sunlight and processing. Different parts of a plant can have varying amounts of the active ingredient.

The formulation of the remedy can also be important. A tincture may have more potency than a pill, or vice versa.

Plants contain many different chemicals, so when you use an herbal remedy you are using a complex mixture of ingredients. This can be positive, since the ingredients may work together, but negative interactions between the chemicals can also occur.

Like prescription medications, herbal remedies have side effects. A formulation that never causes any side effects in anyone probably has no active ingredients. In addition, drug interactions can occur between herbal remedies and prescribed medications.

Many drug interaction problems have been found to be related to an enzyme system in the body called cytochrome P450, a group of chemicals produced in the liver that are involved in breaking down toxins. You may have read about problems with drinking grapefruit juice and taking certain medications. This is because of quercitin, a chemical found in grapefruit juice that inhibits one of the cytochromes. Quercitin is also found in St. John's wort, ginkgo and valerian, all of which have been used in herbal remedies to treat depression and sleep problems. When you take something that inhibits the cytochrome system, your body will respond as if you were taking a higher dose of your medication. This effect can lead to increased levels in the body of tricyclic antidepressants, some antipsychotic medications and even caffeine. Other medications that do not have psychiatric uses can also be affected, so combining alternative depression treatments with conventional medications is not a good idea.

St. John's wort (also St. Johnswort)

Hypericum perforatum, commonly known as St. John's wort, is a perennial herb that grows in Europe and North America. It is said that it is called St. John's wort because its golden-yellow flowers are at their height towards the end of June and, as June 24 is considered to be the birthday of St. John the Baptist, the plant was named after him. It has been used as a folk remedy for a number of ailments, including depression, insomnia, anxiety, mania, syphilis, tuberculosis, pertussis and parasites. As far as I can tell, its current uses are limited to the first four problems, although there has been some research on its antiviral properties.

Hypericum is used widely in Germany as a treatment for mild depression and is gaining popularity in North America. As with synthetic antidepressants, it does not work for everyone and can take up to six weeks for positive effects to become apparent.

Some studies of the effectiveness of this drug are not useful because they have often been done on only small numbers of patients, or because they compare hypericum to very low dosages of antidepressants or to drugs that are not commonly used in depression, such as diazepam. Some of the better trials have been combined and analyzed in a meta-analysis, which showed positive results in the treatment of mild to moderate depression.

A large multicenter research study being conducted on adults in the United States will be finished in 2000 and may yield definitive results. This study will compare three groups, one treated with St. John's wort, one treated with a placebo and one treated with adequate doses of a conventional anti-depressant medication. Another advantage of this study is that after the initial eight-week treatment period, the subjects will be monitored for a further 18 weeks. If the results of this study are positive, we can hope that a large, equally well-designed study of children and teens will follow.

The mechanism of action for St. John's wort is not clear. In fact, a single active ingredient has not been identified, although some research has looked at hypericin, a red pigment in the plant. It has been postulated that it is a natural MAO inhibitor (see page 67), but no reactions to red wine, cheese or chocolate have been reported in people taking it.

It has recently been shown that St. John's wort contains high levels of naturally occurring melatonin. In fact, some St. John's wort pills on the market have more melatonin in them than some melatonin pills. Melatonin is a hormone that seems to regulate the sleeping/waking cycle, and it is being used extensively in the treatment of sleep problems and to prevent jet lag. As sleep difficulties are common with depression, and sleep deprivation may make depression worse, the melatonin in St. John's wort may contribute to its usefulness as a treatment. However, in addition to causing nightmares, melatonin has been reported to cause a worsening of depression, so if St. John's wort were used in someone likely to react in this way to melatonin, its positive effect would be reduced or even reversed.

St. John's wort does seem to have few negative side effects. A large German study reported that fewer than 3 percent of people experienced side effects. As with many drugs, nausea, vomiting and diarrhea were most frequently reported. Some allergic reactions were noted, although none were serious. Fatigue and restlessness also occurred in users.

There is concern that sun exposure while on hypericum could be dangerous. This is based on Australian observations that sheep that eat St. John's wort have died from sun exposure. Although no severe photosensitivity reactions have been reported in humans, it would be wise if your teen took precautions against sun exposure while on St. John's wort. She will be well protected if she wears a hat with a wide brim, long-sleeved shirts and pants and, of course, a sunscreen with a high SPF number (at least 20). Staying out of the sun between noon and three o'clock would also be a reasonable precaution. Suntanning is definitely out, not always an easy thing to sell to teens.

Although some sources feel that it is safe to take St. John's wort in combination with other medications, including antidepressants, I would caution against doing so. Recent reports suggest that St. John's Wort interferes with the absorption of some protease inhibitors, used to treat HIV.

A teen with a mild to moderate depression could try St. John's wort. If he is on another antidepressant, the dosage should be tapered off and stopped completely with a doctor's supervision before he starts St. John's wort. He must have demonstrated that he is committed to "sun safety," and he should continue to be seen by his therapist.

Ginkgo Biloba

Ginkgo biloba is an herbal remedy used by many adults for depression. It is said to improve blood flow to the brain and to have an effect on neurotransmitter levels. The side effects make me wonder if it is mainly a stimulant. High doses (more than 240 mg a day) have been associated with diarrhea, headaches, restlessness and irritability. In addition, ginkgo has anticoagulant effects and can lead to bruising or bleeding, especially if given with other anticoagulants or ASA.

Ginkgo has been used in the treatment of sexual dysfunction (often failure to achieve orgasm) associated with SSRIs. There don't seem to be any controlled studies of this, but many doctors have reported some success.

Conventional Alternatives

Electroconvulsive Therapy (ECT)

Although a "conventional alternative," electroconvulsive therapy (ECT) is controversial. Some treatment centers do not use it at all, and many places use it only for adults. Its use is restricted to fairly specific situations, such as the very suicidal patient whose severe depression has not responded to other forms of treatment, and people with psychotic depression.

The therapy, which uses an electrical current to cause a seizure, was originally developed as a treatment for schizophrenia when it was noticed that schizophrenics tended to improve if they developed epilepsy. This was before antipsychotic drugs were invented. Various ways of inducing seizures were tried, including some medications, but ECT seemed to have the least side effects. ECT was developed in the days when there was no effective drug treatment for any mental illnesses, so it isn't surprising that it was also used for a number of other problems. It became clear that it worked best in people with major depression.

Almost everyone is repelled by the idea of giving someone electric shocks, and movie portrayals of this treatment as it was used decades ago have added to the horror. In addition to this, ECT can have serious side effects, including temporary memory loss and temporary confusion. There can be prolonged seizures and problems with irregular heartbeat (which almost always resolve on their own). Muscle soreness, headaches and nausea are common after treatment. In adults, there are between 2 and 4.5 deaths for every 100,000 ECT treatments, mainly in people with pre-existing heart problems.

No randomized controlled trials (in which patients are randomly assigned to either the group that would get ECT or the group that gets another treatment) have been done on children or teens. Studies in this age group have looked at how well ECT works, and at side effects, but not at more complicated issues like long-term effects on brain development. Many people have wondered whether the electric energy itself or the heat it creates could cause long-term structural brain problem, but neither autopsies nor imaging studies (such as magnetic resonance imaging [MRI] and computerized tomography [CAT]) have shown visible damage from ECT. After ECT, an increase in brain water content has been shown in some studies, but this effect seems to be short-lived. Some previous concerns about long-term memory loss and thinking problems have been laid to rest. In fact, many seriously depressed teens have difficulty thinking and remembering, and these functions often improve after ECT, as the depression lifts.

ECT has a very high success rate and has the advantage of not having to be used on an ongoing basis. Doses used in teens are lower than in adults. The therapy should be used only if recommended and administered by a psychiatrist. Before the first treatment, there should be a full physical examination and some laboratory investigations to make sure the teen is physically healthy.

A short-acting anesthetic is administered to the teen, so all the potential problems of anesthesia must be considered. Muscle relaxation is also induced by a drug so that there are no body spasms during the treatment. Seizure activity is closely monitored throughout the treatment. Oxygen is administered before the treatment, which helps in cutting down on side effects. The teen should have nothing to eat or drink for eight hours before each treatment.

Directing the electric current to only the "non-dominant" side of the brain seems to decrease the chance of memory problems. The data is split on whether this also lessens the therapeutic effect. Wave currents were originally used, but they caused significant memory problems and are now considered to be obsolete. Brief pulse currents are now employed.

A course of ECT usually involves treatments two to three times a week for several weeks, but you may see positive results after only one treatment. If there isn't major improvement after 12 treatments, seek a second opinion from another psychiatrist before continuing.

ECT has been shown to be safe in pregnancy. It is riskier in a number of conditions uncommon in adolescence, such as recent heart attack, severe high blood pressure or retinal detachment. Risk is increased in people who have a brain tumor or any other cause of high pressures in the brain.

At this time, ECT is usually used only in teens with a serious major depression or serious bipolar disorder who are not responding to treatment, or who are very suicidal.

Light Therapy

Bright light has been shown to be an effective treatment for seasonal affective disorder (SAD). While most of the research has been done on adults (most people with SAD are adults), anecdotal evidence suggests that light therapy works for adolescents also. In the areas where SAD is most common, many teens attend schools that have little natural lighting, rarely have gym class outside in the winter and tend to stay at school for lunch, so they get almost no sun exposure during the winter months.

If moving to Cuba isn't an option, artificial light is a good alternative. This treatment, called phototherapy, uses light sources that do not contain the ultraviolet end of the spectrum and so do not cause tanning or burning. You can hope to see rapid improvement in your teen when she is treated with light therapy. The equipment will be prescribed by your doctor and can be rented. Some drug plans will cover all or part of the cost.

The teen needs to be exposed to the light for at least two hours a day at a strength of 2500 lux (a metric measurement of illumination intensity). His eyes should be open but he doesn't have to stare at the lights, so he can have the treatments while reading, doing homework or watching TV. The treatment seems to work best if it takes place in the morning. Research is being done on the application of light to areas of the body that have fairly superficial blood vessels, such as the backs of the knees, but this approach is not in clinical use yet. It is likely that portable phototherapy units that deliver light to the backs of the knees will be developed, but testing will need to be done to determine optimal times and dosages.

For a teen who does not have full-blown seasonal affective disorder but does have winter blues, a one-hour walk at lunch time may have a positive effect, although some of the benefit may be from the exercise itself.

L-tryptophan

Up until the end of the 1980s, L-tryptophan was a commonly used alternative treatment for depression and sleep problems. It is one of the amino acids, which are the building blocks of proteins. Our bodies don't manufacture it; we normally get it from proteins in our food. L-tryptophan is used by the body to manufacture serotonin (see Chapter 3).

L-tryptophan's usefulness in treating depression hasn't been established scientifically, but many people were taking it in the 1980s when a link was discovered between one particular batch of pills and the appearance of a rare blood disorder, eosinophilia-myalgia syndrome, in the people who were treated with these pills. In addition to a laboratory finding of an elevated white blood cell count, symptoms of this disorder include high fever, joint and muscle pain, swelling of the extremities, difficulty in thinking, nerve problems, rashes and even difficulty breathing. A national registry of these patients showed that while about two-thirds of over 200 patients had significant improvement over two years, those who developed decreased mental capabilities actually got worse. In addition, peripheral nerve problems did not seem to improve.

Because of the large number of people experiencing eosinophilia-myalgia syndrome related to taking L-tryptophan, it was taken off the market. It is still available at some health food stores, however, and users take it for depression and sleep problems.

Caffeine

Many of us rely on this drug to get us going at the beginning of the day. Teens tend to get their caffeine from soft drinks, although many are also regular coffee drinkers. In addition to being a stimulant, caffeine seems to have a mood-elevating effect. Although no one recommends caffeine as a treatment for depression, many teens find that consuming it is helpful when they are having a particularly difficult day. Withdrawal symptoms include irritability, depressed mood and headaches, so teens should not suddenly stop their caffeine intake. Overuse can lead to sleep problems, restlessness and tremors.

Homeopathy

The underlying theory of homeopathy is almost the direct opposite of allopathic (conventional) medicine. In homeopathy, disease is treated with extremely small amounts of substances that, at higher doses, cause the same symptoms as the disease. Homeopathic remedies are made by putting a small amount of the substance into purified water and then putting some of the resulting solution into another container of purified water and so on, until there is almost no chance of there being any of the original substance in the solution. The idea is that the water is changed by having had the substance in it at some point. At each dilution, the solution is vigorously shaken (succussed). I have to admit to some skepticism about this. No water can be so purified that there are no other molecules mixed in. How does the solution know which molecules it is supposed to be reacting to?

The activities of each remedy have been determined by volunteers who have taken larger amounts of the substances and closely monitored themselves and noted their symptoms. An assumption is made that all new feelings or symptoms are due to the substance. Homeopathic books list the many remedies with all their resultant symptoms.

The homeopathic practitioner will do a thorough assessment, asking your teen more questions than you can imagine. This professional is not only interested in symptoms, but also in things such as food cravings and dislikes, the preferred temperature for drinks, whether your teen gets hot or cold at night and many other such issues. The homeopath will also do a full physical exam.

The practitioner will then try to find a remedy based on the adolescent's answers. There may be a large number of suggested remedies, or only one or two. Don't just go to the drugstore and buy a homeopathic remedy that is labeled "for depression" or some other symptom. According to homeopathic theory, the remedy will work for your teen only if all the information gleaned from the individual is used to formulate the prescription. The remedy has to suit the whole picture.

A great thing about homeopaths is that they tend to spend quite a bit of time with their patients and pay close attention to what they say. This can be therapeutic in itself, as can the positive and hopeful outlook most homeopaths communicate.

Acupuncture

Acupuncture is an old Chinese healing tool that reputedly changes the energy flow in the body. It has been used for a wide variety of medical conditions. Steel needles are inserted into parts of the body known as acupuncture points. Traditionally, there were fewer than 400 known acupuncture points, but now there are about 2,000 that have been identified. Sometimes a small electrical current is run through the needles. Acupressure is a treatment in which pressure is applied to these points.

A small American study of women with major depression

compared three groups. One group got no acupuncture, one received acupuncture to points that are not supposed to be related to depression and one group were given appropriate acupuncture treatment. The group that got acupuncture to depression points had significant mood elevation in comparison to the other two groups.

Reported adverse effects of acupuncture include fainting, bruising, seizures, punctured lung and nerve damage. Moreover, if the equipment is not properly sterilized, infectious diseases such as hepatitis B and C, as well as HIV (human immunodeficiency virus), can be transmitted.

Aromatherapy

Aromatherapy uses the oils in plants to treat a variety of problems. It is sometimes combined with massage. For many of us, smells evoke strong feelings and sometimes intense memories. Aromatherapists feel that specific essential oils can be used to treat a large variety of illnesses; essential oils have the characteristic odor of the host plant.

Oils that are said to help with depression are grapefruit, ylang-ylang, bergamot (this is the stuff in Earl Grey tea), camomile, geranium, rose and others. One very small Japanese study showed significant improvement in a group of severely depressed adult men who were treated with a strong citrus fragrance daily for several months. I could not find any research on aromatherapy in depressed teens.

Essential oils should not be eaten. When they are used as directed, it is unlikely that they will cause any major adverse effects, although they can cause rashes if applied to the skin. Essential oils are expensive to buy, even in the small quantities used by aromatherapists.

Exercise

People who are mentally healthy tend to be more physically active than those who are not. Either of these states could contribute to the other, so it is difficult to attribute the good mental health to the exercise. Also, overexercising can be associated with poorer mental health.

There is some evidence that regular exercise can aid recovery from depression. A large study in California showed relief of depression in people who became physically active. This beneficial result may be due to increased levels of endorphins in individuals who exercise. Endorphins, chemicals made by the body, are similar to morphine and can induce a feeling of well-being. It could also be that the depressed teen feels better about herself because she pushed herself to get out and exercise. She may feel less out of control when she is focusing on things other than her depression, and may also meet people and interact with them as part of the exercise experience. Activities such as yoga may help alleviate feelings of anxiety or restlessness that can accompany a depression.

The exercise does not have to be vigorous. Both strenuous and more gentle exercise has been shown to have a good effect. Teens can pick activities at which they are likely to succeed. It may be easier to do an exercise that does not require travel or a special membership. Jumping rope, walking, bike riding or blading may appeal to a teen. On the other hand, if they are motivated, an exercise class or team activity would provide a social component that may be lacking in some other activities.

Don't expect results overnight. Just as the effects of anti-depressant medication can take weeks to appear, the benefits of exercise will likely take a while to show themselves.

Massage

Massage helps people relax. It helps them feel attended to and cared for. Physical contact with other people is comforting, but a depressed teen who has withdrawn from friends and family may not be getting her usual amount of hugs and pats. A teen who is feeling socially isolated and lonely may feel better after a massage because she has had some personal physical contact.

A massage is also a good time for a teen to experience his body in a positive manner. Depression often carries with it a feeling of heaviness in the body, aches and pains and a lack of joyful physical experiences. A massage may help him realize that he will not always feel so bad, both in his body and his soul.

Pastoral Counseling

A number of ministers, priests and rabbis provide counseling to members of their congregations. This counseling may or may not include prayer or other overt spiritual content. There has been increasing interest in the role of prayer in recovery from illness, but I have been unable to find any research about its effects for teens with depression. There is a centuries-long traditional precedent for the practice of counseling by religious guides. A teen with spiritual leanings might do well with this kind of approach, although if it isn't helpful she might feel abandoned by God, which could make things worse. Parents should check out a pastoral counselor the same way they would screen any therapist.

Diet and Dietary Supplements

Practitioners in a number of fields feel that mental illness is a result of dietary imbalances. Good nutrition is important to health, but it is unlikely that many teen depressions are caused by poor nutrition.

Vitamin supplements may be suggested for a teen with depression. Some vitamins can cause health problems if taken in large amounts, but with most vitamins, the body uses what it needs and gets rid of the rest, so a trial of vitamin supplements is unlikely to hurt.

Some of my patients who have taken vitamins for depression seem to have been given B vitamins or a mixture of many vitamins and minerals. Vitamin B_6 may be linked to serotonin availability. Small doses (10 mg/day) have been shown in some small, adult studies to result in improved mood. Folic acid, which is being added to flour in many countries, has also been shown to help in some small studies.

There seems to be little research in the area of teens, depression and vitamins. I am somewhat suspicious of practitioners who sell vitamins or other supplements to their patients, and would be more likely to trust someone who isn't making a profit from the recommendations.

I am also leery of extreme diets for the treatment of depression. Teens need a wide variety of foods from all food groups and plenty of calories, especially while they are growing. A practitioner who decides the teen is allergic to everything except rice and meat will, for example, suggest a diet that is deficient in many nutrients, including vitamins.

Doing for Others

I haven't been able to locate any research on this, but I am convinced that volunteer work can be a useful adjunct to depression treatment. It can be difficult for a depressed teen to mobilize herself to get involved with volunteer work, but when she does, it often provides new meaning to her life. She may be exposed to, and inspired by, people who are very hopeful despite difficult life events. She may become quite busy with this work, distracting herself from her problems. She will meet new people and broaden her horizons.

Parents can help by calling various agencies and finding out their requirements for volunteer work. A depressed teen may feel overwhelmed working directly with clients of an agency, but might be happy packing groceries for a food bank or doing secretarial work for an AIDS organization, daycare center or seniors' home.

One pitfall to watch for is that depressed teens may feel guilty that they feel bad, when they have "so much" compared to the people they are serving.

Talk to Your Doctor First

Some of the treatments described above can be used along with traditional therapy and, whether or not they work as promised, they may give the teen a feeling that she is taking control over her depression. However, teens should not stop or add to their regular treatment without a discussion with their doctor or therapist. Most treatments I've described do not have serious side effects when taken in recommended doses, other than depleting the bank account.

7. Substance Abuse and Depression

Substance abuse and depression are often seen together in teens. For example, when teens get drunk, they often feel excited, stimulated and euphoric. Later in the evening (if they haven't passed out), they may feel depressed and irritable. It is interesting that these negative feelings and the hangover the following morning do not deter many teens from continuing to drink. This is partly because drinking is a very social activity, and teens may not want to lose the benefits associated with being part of a group. Also, they may be looking for the relaxed feeling they get while becoming drunk. However, if they start to drink frequently, they may develop symptoms of depression that persist between the drinking bouts and find that drinking no longer provides a lift. Parents who are not aware of their teen's alcohol use may see that their teen is depressed, but may not realize that this depression is secondary to alcohol abuse.

Teens who are heavy users of alcohol, cigarettes or marijuana are more likely to be depressed than those who are moderate, light or non-users of these drugs. There are a number of theories about why this is so. One theory suggests that depressed teens drink or take other drugs in an attempt to improve their mood, in effect, treating themselves for depression. Another proposes that a tendency to substance abuse is genetically linked with a tendency to depression. Other theories postulate that the same personality, familial and cultural factors that contribute to depression may also be linked to substance abuse. Some researchers believe that substance use causes depressive disorders. It is likely that all of these are true to some extent.

Substance use as self-treatment does not usually work. The teen may experience temporary relief from depressed feelings, but this relief is usually short-lived. Some drugs may help with specific symptoms, like marijuana increasing appetite. But these drugs do not cure depression; in fact, they may make depression worse, may make academic difficulties worse and may even increase the risk of suicide.

Dangerous Interactions

A combination of substance use and depression can lead to dangerous interactions between prescribed medications, drugs and alcohol. There may also be problems with a teen remembering (or bothering) to take his medication while stoned. Teens cannot effectively participate in therapy while inebriated. A teen may use substances to deal with a depression himself, thus delaying treatment. Some substances may make a depression worse. Most important is the link between suicide, depression and substance use. A depressed teen's alcohol use over a period of time and his actually being drunk both increase the risk of suicide.

Some drugs have effects that mimic depression. It can be difficult to determine whether a teen is depressed and abusing substances or has depressive symptoms as a result of substance use. This is a situation where a doctor's help should be sought sooner rather than later. Depressed mood can result from prescribed medication as well as from illicit substances—parents are not always aware that their children have been prescribed a drug and may not get an honest answer to a question about medication use, such as when the teen is taking birth control pills. Depression has been associated with beta blockers (drugs used to prevent migraines, for some anxiety problems and other conditions) and with some heart medication.

The teen may start using drugs before a depression occurs, and the two may not be directly connected. Some illicit drugs can cause feelings of sadness, and withdrawal from them can lead to a feeling of depression. In a teen with a pre-existing depression, drugs can worsen the situation.

The highest rates of depression co-existing with substance abuse seem to occur in people with bipolar disorder, almost seven times the rate of substance abuse in the general population and two to three times higher than in people with other types of depression.

Substance abuse can actually precipitate the first episode of manic depression. It can worsen pre-existing bipolar disorder by increasing the frequency of the cycles of mania and depression. It has been noted that people with bipolar disorder often use drugs that make their current state more exaggerated (like cocaine while manic and alcohol while depressed), which would suggest that substance use in these teens is not a type of self-medication.

Use of alcohol and cigarettes is high in teens, while use of other drugs is much less common. Many teens experiment with substances or even go on to use them fairly regularly, without any resulting difficulties. Teens with depression are more likely to go on to problem drug use.

Teens who are depressed and using alcohol or other drugs

should get treatment from a person or program skilled in dealing with both issues. As the mental health and drug treatment systems are separate entities in most places, this combination of skills can be hard to find.

Teens who are less vulnerable to problem drug use include those with higher intelligence, higher self-esteem, strong family support, good social skills and good problem-solving skills. Some of these factors also protect teens from depression.

How to Tell If Your Depressed Teen Is Using Drugs

As mentioned above, it can be difficult to tell if a depressed adolescent is taking drugs, as many of the typical signs of problem drug use are similar to those of depression. Poor academic performance, memory and concentration difficulties and a change in appetite and weight are some of the signs that are similar.

The argument has been made that since many teens experiment with drugs and few go on to have serious drug problems, parents do not really need to try to "catch" their children taking drugs. However, with a depressed teen, the consequences of drug use, especially alcohol, can be major, so parents who suspect that their depressed adolescent is taking drugs should seek help right away.

The two most commonly abused drugs in adolescence, alcohol and nicotine, have the advantage from the parents' point of view of being detectable by smell. Of course, many teens who smoke say they smell like smoke because their friends smoke and the smell gets on their clothes. If your teen comes in after you have gone to bed, you will be less likely to detect the smell of alcohol, as it will be out of his system by morning.

There are not very many physical signs of drug use. Your teen's fingers may be stained from nicotine, eyes bloodshot from marijuana. Although there can be many causes of a chronic cough, like asthma, it may be associated with smoking. Similarly, a runny nose could be caused by allergies or a cold that won't let go, but it may also be caused by cocaine or heroin use.

Psychological changes in your teen may also be a sign of drug use but are very non-specific. They include loss of enjoyment in life and activities, withdrawal and irritability. Social changes might include dropping an old group and making new, often older, friends. The substance-using depressed teen might show an exaggeration of symptoms. If he was irritable before, he might become verbally abusive or even physically destructive. Mood swings may become much more pronounced. Periods of social withdrawal may become longer. Appetite changes that are a result of the depression may reverse when the teen starts taking drugs, so a teen who wasn't eating may turn into one who is eating all the time. Any unexpected change, such as a depression getting worse while the teen is receiving adequate treatment, can also be a warning sign.

None of these signs are specific, but even if they are not associated with substance use, many of them are cause for concern. Your teen may not respond honestly to a question about substance use, even if you ask in a non-accusatory way, but it is still worth asking and talking about the negative effects of drug and alcohol use during depression.

What to Do If Your Teen Is Using Drugs

The first thing to do if you find out your teen is using drugs is calm down. It is not useful to scream, blame, rant or rave, as tempting as these responses might be. Talk to your teen about what you have found out. Let your teen know how you are feeling (angry, disappointed, betrayed, sad, embarrassed ...). Let him know that you are willing to help and to work towards rebuilding trust. Acknowledge that you understand that drugs might have given him relief from his depression, but that this is not a viable solution to his problems.

Two sources of immediate help might be your teen's therapist and his doctor. They may be prepared to deal with issues around substance abuse, or may feel he needs to see someone with more expertise. Most experts in this area work as part of a team, so be prepared to look for a substance abuse program. The therapist, the doctor or possibly a school counselor may know about programs and be able to recommend one. You need to check out the program yourself and make sure that counselors are both skilled with teens and knowledgeable about issues of depression.

What to Look for in a Substance Abuse Program

If you are looking for a treatment program for your teen, you will find there are a number of options, including in-patient, residential, day treatment and outpatient programs. These are run by a variety of groups, some of them non-profit.

Programs that mix adults and teens are not a good idea. The issues that these two groups are dealing with are often different, and adult viewpoints are different from those of teens. Whoever is running these programs needs a good understanding of adolescent development, something that is not often found in people who were trained to work with adults.

The program should be able to deal with a teen who is depressed and substance-abusing. Neither problem should be ignored or seen as less important than the other. You should ask the people who run these programs how many teens with depression they treat in a year and what their approach is. However, beware of a program where everyone has two diagnoses. Some American programs get paid for in-patient or residential treatment of substance abuse patients only if they have more than one problem. These for-profit programs then make sure they have diagnosed everyone with an additional psychiatric problem, such as depression. One way to spot a program like this may be the high percentage of patients for whom lithium is prescribed.

By the time a teen gets substance abuse treatment, the family may have been disrupted and family therapy could be beneficial. Support groups can be helpful to parents, but cannot replace family therapy. A program should provide both family and individual counseling, even if every patient does not need both. Many programs also offer group therapy, or training in social skills and problem solving.

Although some good programs are sponsored by religious groups, the treatment should not require joining a religion, nor should the treatment involve religion. Recognizing the spiritual aspect of a teen's life is appropriate, as long as it does not involve conversion.

No program in the world can cure all the teens it treats, so if the people who run a program make promises that seem unrealistic, ask to see the figures. They may show that at the time of discharge everyone has been "clean" for a certain period of time, but this does not always predict success outside. Ask to see one-year follow-up rates and find out what percentage of kids were left out because they were "lost to follow-up" or dropped out of the program.

Abstinence-based programs can be a setup for disaster. If

the only success is considered to be staying away from all drugs all the time, most teens will fail, if not while in intensive treatment, then after. Programs that help the teen figure out the most dangerous or bothersome aspects of the problem and then address them are more likely to succeed because the work is done in smaller chunks, with each success increasing the teen's self-confidence and willingness to attack more of the problem. Of course, abstinence as a goal is most important with the most dangerous drugs.

Not only should counselors be sensitive to cultural, racial, sexual orientation and socio-economic issues, the program's mission statement and rules should also reflect this.

Some people in the substance abuse field feel that everyone with a problem should be involved with a "step program," on the Alcoholics Anonymous model. Many teens deal with their drug or alcohol problems without one of these groups. Teens who are looking for a highly structured program may benefit from the AA model, but others should not be forced to attend such a group.

When assessing a program's suitability for your teen, ask yourself: Do the counselors in the program seem to actually like the teens? Is there an atmosphere of mutual respect? Both of these aspects are important, although the counselors should not come across as buddies to the patients. If you see teens and counselors smoking together outside, for example, it may mean that the boundaries between the two are blurred.

Find out if the program is willing to use medication for depression. Some substance abuse programs have a "chemical-free" policy that does not allow psychiatric medications on the grounds that they are drugs. This can delay improvement or even cause a teen to abandon the program.

Specific Substances

Alcohol

Alcohol is a commonly used drug in adolescence, with a strong link to adolescent deaths from motor vehicle, boating and diving accidents, and from suicide. Other associated risks include sexual assault, hypothermia and disabilities resulting from accidents or suicide attempts. I am amazed at the number of 14- and 15-year-olds who tell me they "only drink socially." Some of their parents will even buy beer for teen parties, saying that it is safer for them to drink at home than somewhere else.

There seems to be a genetic predisposition to severe alcohol problems; some studies show a gender association, with fathers and sons having the highest risk. The familial link between alcohol abuse and depression is more controversial, with some studies finding that families with depressed members have a high chance of also having members with alcohol-related problems. Other studies have failed to duplicate these findings. Having a parent with a drinking problem certainly creates a risk that the kids will become depressed, including a higher likelihood of physical and emotional abuse, poverty and neglect.

There is no doubt that drinking is a dangerous activity in depressed teens. Teens who are depressed, drinking and have a firearm in the home are at very high risk of suicide.

Nicotine

One of the more interesting links in the area of substance abuse and depression is the connection between cigarette smoking and depression.

The evidence shows that smokers are more likely to exhibit depressive symptoms than non-smokers, and that major depression is also more common in smokers. Non-depressed teens who smoke are more likely than those who don't smoke to become depressed adults.

Moreover, smokers with a history of depression, compared with smokers who have never had a major depression, are twice as likely to fail at attempts to stop smoking. And smokers who quit are more likely to become depressed than those who don't.

Cytochromes are chemicals in the liver that metabolize drugs and seem to be involved with the ability to metabolize nicotine. One genetic variant in part of this system produces people who are less likely to smoke and, if they do, they smoke less. If the system processes nicotine poorly, the higher levels of nicotine in the blood may lead to an exaggeration of its effects, perhaps discouraging a teen from trying smoking again. A version of the gene that leads to more efficient metabolism of nicotine (which would be associated with a higher risk of smoking) might also result in lower levels of other chemicals, such as neurotransmitters, perhaps resulting in depression.

Is nicotine, or some other agent in cigarette smoke, an antidepressant? If the answer to this question is yes, it's possible that depressed people smoke because it makes them feel better. Another possibility is that the newly discovered gene that makes some people dislike smoking, or at least never really get hooked, also helps them to resist depression. People lacking the gene, in this theory, would be more susceptible to depression. We don't know the answers to these questions yet, but we do know that one antidepressant, buproprion, also decreases the craving for nicotine, thus reducing smoking. So whatever the link between smoking and depression, buproprion is one medication that has been shown to be helpful for both.

Caffeine

Although we don't tend to think about coffee, tea and soft drinks when dealing with the issue of adolescent substance use, many teens do consume caffeine, sometimes heavily. Many are not even aware they're using caffeine when they consume colas, root beer and other soft drinks.

Young people take to caffeine for a number of reasons. This is the stage of life when people start to realize there are not enough hours in the day. Teens drink caffeine-containing beverages in the evenings so they can stay up late to finish assignments or study for exams. They drink them during the day to help stay alert and awake after a night of partying. They may actually take caffeine directly, in pill form, when they feel a strong need to stay awake. Some young women who have weight issues take caffeine to dull their appetite.

Caffeine has significant positive effects. In addition to reducing fatigue, it can increase the ability to focus on a task, increase energy, improve self-confidence and mood and endow the user with a feeling of well-being. Teens who are depressed may benefit from these effects and unconsciously increase their caffeine intake. If caffeine is suddenly withdrawn, such as when the young person goes to summer camp, there could be a sharp increase in depressive symptoms.

Heavy coffee drinking is associated with a high alcohol intake and heavy cigarette smoking, and some studies have shown that coffee drinkers are more likely to report high levels of stress both at work and at home. Yet despite these risk factors, heavy coffee drinkers are significantly less likely to commit suicide than their light- or non-coffee-drinking counterparts.

However, the side effects of high levels of caffeine intake can include agitation, tremors and even paranoid thinking. Moderate levels of caffeine intake have not been shown to be dangerous, but more than three or four cups of coffee a day should be discouraged.

Ecstasy

Ecstasy is a drug that became popular at raves (large, all-night, usually alcohol-free parties, often held in warehouses) and was believed to be relatively safe at first. Reports of severe heart problems resulting from Ecstasy use began to emerge a few years after its consumption became widespread.

Ecstasy might seem to be the perfect drug to someone who is depressed. It leads to an energized, often joyful state that is the opposite of depression. However, recent evidence suggests that this drug kills brain cells that produce serotonin. Low levels of serotonin are associated with depression. You can picture a depressed teen taking Ecstasy more and more often, only to feel increasingly depressed in between. It seems likely that these brain changes are not reversible, as dead brain cells are not replaced.

The Good News

Most teens with depression do not abuse drugs. Some try alcohol or marijuana but feel worse and so don't try it again. Others don't have the energy even to experiment.

Teens with untreated depression may end up getting help because of their drug use or because a parent, seeing the signs of depression as signs of drug use, intervenes.

More and more, those who design programs for teens are realizing that their counselors need to be able to recognize and treat both depression and substance use, and these counselors are providing the type of care that will help these teens feel much better.

8. Anxiety Disorders and Depression

Sophie is an outgoing 12-year-old. She does well in school and has lots of friends. She has never wanted to go to a sleepover and usually her friends come to her house to play, but she also goes to their houses. Last summer, Sophie was invited to a friend's cottage for a weekend and was excited about going. She had a great time swimming and playing on Saturday, but when bedtime came, she started to feel nervous. She lay in bed, her heart pounding, all kinds of thoughts going through her head. What if her parents had been killed in a car accident? Maybe she would never see them again. After two hours, she got up and told one of the adults that she wanted to go home. They tried to console her, but she started to cry and couldn't stop. The adults called her parents, but she could hardly talk to them. In the end they drove up to get her.

Sophie's parents took her to an anxiety clinic for children and teens. At the clinic, she was taught a number of strategies to deal with separation and then she practiced these strategies, going to a friend's house until midnight and then working up to staying overnight. Sophie still feels a bit uncomfortable when she is away from home all night, but this summer she went back to her friend's cottage and was able to stay.

Anxiety is not the same as depression, though the two can and often do co-exist. Sophie's problem is a common one in childhood and adolescence, encompassing a range of difficulties that includes fear of animals, fear of the dark or being alone, obsessive-compulsive disorder, school avoidance, panic attacks and extreme homesickness. Some teens have an anxious temperament (they are often described by their parents as worriers), but the line between an anxious temperament and an anxiety disorder is clear: if it does not affect their ability to function, it's not a disorder. Many teens keep their feelings of anxiety to themselves. It can take astute parents to detect moderate levels of anxiety in their adolescent child.

Depressed teens are much more likely to have an anxiety disorder than teens who aren't depressed. Some teens swing between the two. When the conditions co-exist, the teen tends to do poorly in school and tends not to function well socially. It has been shown that adults who have both depression and anxiety experience more severe depression and more difficulty recovering than those who suffer from depression only. These adults are also twice as likely to attempt suicide as those with anxiety disorders only. Treatment for adults and teens often seems to focus on the depression, but it is important to address the anxiety also, as this will lead to improved social functioning and perhaps even prevent the recurrence of the depression. Some theorists feel that anxiety disorders and depression are part of one illness, with the two conditions having neurophysiological and psychological causes in common, and a large area of overlap.

Parents may take some comfort in knowing that there is a growing body of literature showing that anxious teens are less likely to get into trouble with the law or to abuse alcohol or drugs. This makes sense, as the teen's anxiety probably prevents him from taking extreme risks.

All anxiety disorders involve problems with behavior and thought (such as irrational fears or obsessions) and are often accompanied by physiological changes (such as a rapid heartbeat, hyperventilation, nausea, sweating, blushing or shakiness in the hands or voice).

From a developmental point of view, fears and worries are a normal part of growing up. Anxiety is a common, basic emotion. Although it is an uncomfortable thing to experience, it warns us to be careful in new or unusual situations. The physiological changes noted above are part of the classic "fight or flight" phenomenon, in which the body gears up to deal with a challenge. Separation anxiety is an essential part of life from the time a baby learns that he is a separate being from his parents, at about seven or eight months, until the age of six or so.

It is not uncommon for a young adolescent to have bedtime fears necessitating careful positioning of bedroom or closet doors. Fears and worries about death are also common in the first few years of adolescence. With the young teen's increasing sophistication of thinking, death takes on new meanings and the teen may face the idea of her own mortality for the first time.

Anxiety is part of the cycle of development. A teen facing a new challenge usually accepts a certain level of anxiety as normal and adjusts his behavior to deal with the situation. If things work out well, he experiences less or no anxiety the next time the situation arises. Teens feel better about themselves and move on developmentally after successfully facing a challenge.

A number of anxiety problems have been defined. A certain degree of overlap exists between them, and it can sometimes be hard to tell which applies. The anxious teen who isn't going to school may be experiencing separation anxiety (not wanting to be away from parents) or school phobia (fear of a possible situation at school). If she is trying to avoid a panic attack where one occurred before, she may have a panic disorder. If she is skipping school to avoid a presentation or sport event, it may be social phobia.

What Causes Anxiety Disorders?

Theories about the causes of anxiety disorders center on biological, psychological and social factors.

Studies of twins have shown that a genetic predisposition to anxiety disorders exists. In one of the large twin studies (over 1,000 pairs of female twins) there was found to be a common genetic factor in generalized anxiety disorder and depression. Moreover, because anxiety may be genetically linked, it is not uncommon for an anxious parent to have an anxious child. Each can end up unwittingly contributing to the other's anxiety, and may end up almost glued together by their problems. Treating the anxiety can help them get unstuck.

In addition, there are clearly children (as many as 15 percent) who are born with an anxious or irritable temperament. They tend to become cautious worriers who do not like new situations and are usually fairly quiet. Not all (or even most) of these children get anxiety disorders, and many children with anxiety disorders grow up to be sociable, outgoing, vocal adults.

From a biological point of view, many of the symptoms of anxiety stem from the activation of the sympathetic nervous system. This system partially controls involuntary body functions. Two neurotransmitters, epinephrine and norepinephrine (also called adrenaline and noradrenaline), are the main stimulants of this system. When the levels of these chemicals rise, the heart rate increases, blood is rerouted to vital organs and muscles, the respiratory rate goes up, pupils dilate and sweating increases. It is possible that people with anxiety problems have disturbances in other neurotransmitters that lead to increased epinephrine and norepinephrine levels, or that they are more sensitive to the effects of these neurotransmitters. There may also be some other biological basis for their anxiety. We do know that anxiety problems often respond to SSRIs, but whether this is because of a direct effect on epinephrine and norepinephrine, or because of serotonin effects, is unknown.

New psychological theories propose that anxiety comprises both feeling and thinking components. A teen who believes he can't predict or control events begins to feel helpless. Since a feeling of helplessness is a key part of depression, some psychologists think that anxiety and depression are just at different points of the same spectrum, with the major difference being that an anxious teen may still believe that he can or should control thoughts and feelings. His failure to achieve this leads to agitated bodily feelings. In contrast, a depressed teen feels he has no possibility of control, and his feelings of resigned helplessness lead to a more passive mood and actions.

These theories look at the importance of early life events, especially the baby's control, or lack of it, over her environment. If communication between parent and infant is poor, the baby's emotional experience is one of powerlessness: she has no control because her messages are not being understood and acted upon. In a teen with a biologic predisposition to anxiety and these early childhood experiences of powerlessness, stressful events could trigger an anxiety response.

The most useful therapies for anxiety disorders seem to be the ones that take a practical approach to the problem.

Cognitive therapy has been tailored to deal with these issues, and anxiety specialists who use these therapies are often successful.

Therapy is not always enough. A number of medications (mainly SSRIs) have been shown to be useful in treating anxiety in adults. These drugs are often tried on teens, although I do not know of any controlled trials in anxious teens.

Types of Anxiety Disorders

Separation Anxiety

Sophie, whose story was told at the beginning of this chapter, suffered from separation anxiety. Although it is unusual for a teen who has never had any anxiety problems to develop separation anxiety, it can happen. The depressed, non-anxious teen may show a reluctance to go out, and may miss school, but he is not actually *afraid* of these activities, and will not show the extreme attachment to a parent that the teen with anxiety will exhibit. Teens without previous separation problems tend to have school refusal as their main symptom of separation anxiety.

Separation anxiety can be precipitated by a major life change such as moving or starting a new school. It may follow the death of a family member. Some teens develop this problem after being home sick for a period of weeks or months (as with mononucleosis).

The teen with separation anxiety may be extremely distressed by even the idea of being away from home or her parents. She tends to avoid situations where separation will occur and may function poorly when she is separated from her parents. She worries that her parents will die while she is apart from them or that some other calamity will befall them.

In milder cases, the teen may want to be able to call his parents from school or a party to reassure himself that everything is all right. He may demand an exact schedule of where his parents will be at all times, and it can be hard for him to leave the house in the morning.

The teen with severe anxiety problems may refuse to go to parties or any activity that involves leaving his home for more than a few hours. He will not sleep over at a friend's house. One of the first things a parent might notice in a younger teen is that his child has started to follow him from room to room, or call out for him if things have been quiet for more than a few minutes. He may want to climb onto a parent's lap, something most teens don't do. The most severely affected teens will not go to school, or will leave but then come home early. They are desperate to get out of any situation that involves separation and will go to great lengths to be reunited with their parents. Parents may wake in the morning to find their teen sleeping on the floor beside their bed. I have noticed that teens with the most severe separation anxiety tend to dress like younger children and behave towards their parents in a distinctly non-adolescent, more childlike manner.

Teens with separation anxiety seem more comfortable being home alone, especially if they know where their parents are, than preteens do.

The teen may be "too sick" in the morning to go to school, often with a stomachache or headache. She may put a hot washcloth on her forehead to mimic a fever or run the thermometer under hot water. A teen may beg and cry to be allowed to stay home. The teen who is also depressed is even more likely to have physical problems, such as aches and pains, as a major part of her anxiety.

When the anxiety seems really bad, parents often look back and try to see how things could have deteriorated so much without their really noticing. But separation anxiety tends to creep up on a family, starting with behavior that is within the normal range, such as not wanting to go for sleepovers or calling parents occasionally to say hi. Each progression adds only a small increment of separation anxiety.

Teens who suffer from separation anxiety usually have good social skills and are happy to have friends over to the house. However, friendships often suffer as the teen misses out on important occasions and goes to school less and less. Missing school has major consequences. Teens who are away a lot lose many informal educational experiences that take place before and after classes, in the hallways and in clubs and on teams. Teens with separation anxiety often become physically unfit, as they are not participating in school sports activities. Correspondence courses cannot take the place of a regular school experience.

Although many large cities have anxiety clinics for children and teens, it can be hard to find treatment in smaller centers. However, a child with a mild separation problem will often improve without treatment. He can try strategies aimed at self-reassurance, such as carrying around a little notebook in which he has written messages to himself like "My parents are fine right now" or "I can cope with this situation a little longer—I've done it before." But a teen who is refusing to go to school at all is unlikely to recover without some intervention. Getting her back to school quickly is part of the treatment (the longer she stays away, the less likely it becomes that she will recover). However, sending an anxious teen back to school is difficult—she may see it as a betrayal, as forcing her to be miserable. Lots of support from friends and professionals—for both the teen and the parent—is essential.

A teen who has recovered needs to be aware that there is a chance the problem will return, especially around high-risk times like the end of summer holidays or at the start of high school.

Obsessive-Compulsive Disorder

Bill's parents got a call from the school complaining that he was late almost every day. They couldn't understand it—he often left quite early for junior high. When they talked to him about it, he said he didn't know why he was late, but maybe he was day-dreaming. The next morning his mother watched as he walked down the street. He did seem to be moving slowly and he touched every board on their picket fence as he walked by. He also leaned over and touched the sidewalk once in front of every house. She had never noticed him doing anything like this at home. She called the family doctor who said that Bill might have obsessive-compulsive disorder.

Obsessions are intrusive, recurrent and persistent thoughts, impulses or images. They go beyond excessive worries about real life problems and don't have a strong basis in reality. For instance, a teen whose parent has cancer is not having obsessive thoughts when he finds himself frequently worrying about his parent dying, but a teen whose mother has a cold and who has persistent thoughts that her mother really has cancer may be obsessing.

Common obsessions in teens involve worries about contagious diseases or other contamination and religious, sexual and violent images. I have seen teens who are terrified of getting AIDS come to our clinic for regular testing despite a total absence of any risky behaviors—they aren't even having sex.

Compulsions are behaviors that the teen feels driven to

perform. He may have intricate rules that apply to these behaviors, believing that the behavior will prevent a terrible event from occurring. These behaviors do not normally prevent such an event. Common compulsions are handwashing and other bathing rituals, counting objects and arranging things in a specific pattern. If the pattern, counting or handwashing ritual is not perfect, the teen feels compelled to go back and start over again.

We all get the occasional obsession or compulsion, like a tune from a commercial that repeats over and over in our head. To be classified as a disorder, obsessions and compulsions must cause considerable distress for the child, occupy more than an hour a day or significantly interfere with school or social functioning.

Younger children normally engage in ritual behavior, often around bedtime, with dolls put into their special places, certain words or phrases parents have to say, lights on or off, the door shut or open. These rituals can frequently be modified according to circumstances, and although children may object to changes, they are unlikely to become distraught. These normal rituals tend to fade and are usually gone by age ten. This is the age when obsessive-compulsive disorder (OCD) is the most likely to start (although it can start in adolescence). Boys seem to get OCD earlier than girls do, but by adolescence there is no gender difference. Teens with OCD are at higher risk of depression than their peers. The younger the child at the time OCD develops, the worse the depression seems to be.

Compulsive behaviors in the morning can significantly slow a teen down getting out the door, and parents may think that separation anxiety is developing. Teens may not be willing to discuss compulsions, but parents may notice them touching certain things in the house in a particular order or surreptitiously wiping off the telephone receiver before using it. Red, cracked hands can be a sign of frequent handwashing.

A large proportion of teens with OCD have significant problems with life functioning. Peers may think they are weird, or they may be so embarrassed by their compulsions that they avoid social situations, fearing they will be exposed. Sleepovers become a problem if the teen has a prolonged bedtime or morning ritual. Some rituals have to be performed at home, and the teen will get anxious if she isn't there at the right time. Obsessions and compulsions can distract the teen from schoolwork, so he misses important information while performing a ritual. Some rituals revolve around academics, with repeated checking and rechecking of work to be turned in, obsessive thoughts becoming paralyzing during an exam, multiple-choice answer sheets having to "look" right or avoidance of questions with certain numbers.

Teens with OCD have a great deal of difficulty developing their independence skills. Their social problems may mean that they don't have friends to be independent with. Autonomous acts may lead to feelings of anxiety, which may increase the obsessions and compulsions. Rituals may depend on being near parents or the house.

OCD can be difficult to treat, and many teens continue to have symptoms even after they no longer meet criteria for diagnosis. Most teens can expect substantial improvement with treatments that include medication and cognitive-behavioral therapy.

Social Phobia

When she was 14, Liz moved from a small middle school to a large high school. She had always done well academically, and her parents were pleased with the grades she received on research papers and tests in her various classes. They were surprised when her report card from her new school showed much lower marks in geography, history and English than they had expected. She told them that each of these courses had 20 to 30 percent of the final mark based on oral presentations and that she just "froze up" when she had to get up in front of the class and talk. She was sure she would be laughed at, either because of what she said or how she looked. She had even skipped classes on days when there were to be oral presentations.

Social phobia is a fear of being embarrassed by one's behavior in public or social situations. A teen who suffers from social phobia will not usually realize that her fear is irrational. To be diagnosed, the problem must interfere with functioning or involve severe distress, and must persist for at least six months.

Social phobia is a problem that tends to start in adolescence and is only rarely diagnosed in children under ten. Teens with social phobia are more likely to become depressed than teens without this problem. Such teens were often shy children and now may be afraid of being with unfamiliar adults or teens. Sometimes they are described as loners.

Performance situations, such as giving a class presentation, can be terrifying. Group activities like class projects, gym classes and eating in the cafeteria are also difficult for these teens. If they can, they walk home for lunch or go to a park. If they have to stay on school grounds, they often skip eating and go to the library or another spot where they can be alone. These teens may also skip school or stay home frequently with headaches, stomachaches or other physical complaints. Needless to say, they don't join clubs or play team sports. They are unlikely to date, and even things like ordering food at a fast-food restaurant can be beyond their capabilities.

Teens with social phobia worry about their appearance, but may be afraid to dress fashionably for fear of getting it wrong. They hate changing in front of other people.

In difficult situations these teens tend to focus on their fears and worry about physical reactions like blushing, sweating or shaking. If they speak at all they are likely to make self-deprecating remarks like "You must think I'm an idiot," or apologize unnecessarily.

As with the other anxiety problems discussed, academic function can be affected by missing school and avoiding group activities. Also, fears of embarrassment can be such a large focus during class time that the teen cannot concentrate on either the teacher's remarks or class activities.

Both medication and therapy, especially cognitive-behavioral approaches, are used for this problem.

Other Phobias

Jean is a 14-year-old who was always outgoing, active and upbeat. Four months ago, after reading about the importance of learning the Heimlich maneuver, she suddenly became afraid of choking. She started to worry more and more about it. At first, she chewed her food more carefully, to the point where it was taking her much longer to eat than her younger sister. She wouldn't talk at the table for fear of inhaling a particle of food while distracted. After about a month, she started putting her food in the blender, but even that worried her, as there were sometimes small chunks left. She tried going to school without bringing a lunch, but her mother wouldn't let her, so she threw her lunch out instead. By this time she was losing weight. A friend saw her tossing her lunch in the garbage one day and called Jean's mother, saying that she was worried that Jean had anorexia nervosa. Her mother had been wondering about this also and took Jean to a special program for teens with eating disorders, where her phobia was diagnosed.

Although young children often have fears that seem irrational to adults, phobias go beyond the level of these fears. A teen with a phobia is usually afraid of just one thing. To be diagnosed, the fear must affect functioning or cause marked distress, and it must persist for at least six months (although certainly no one would have refused to treat Jean with her four-month history).

Phobias can develop in childhood, adolescence or adulthood. Most phobic teens are afraid of things that they think will hurt them, like choking, being killed in a plane crash, bleeding to death or being bitten by an animal. In addition to being scared when faced with the phobic object or when there is a reasonable chance that she will be faced with it, the teen will worry irrationally about exposure. She might think, "What if a blind student starts attending my school and has a guide dog and it bites me?"

Teens try to avoid whatever they are afraid of, which may involve changing their route home from school, suggesting going to a mall instead of to a friend's house, or staying home if the weather looks bad. When they come into contact with the phobic object, even in a safe situation, their heart races and they sweat, shake or feel nauseated.

Some phobic stimuli are easy for a teen to avoid, such as snakes or airplanes. Others, especially natural phenomena, are more difficult. Certain situations may unavoidably increase exposure. A healthy teen who is afraid of needles has few shots to deal with and may manage to avoid them, but if he develops a major medical problem, he will have to deal with needles frequently. Parents may not realize how severe their teen's phobia is until they see him in tears or in a rage, when he is forced to confront it. Teens who are afraid of needles often faint when they have blood taken or get injections.

Specific phobias are highly treatable by mental health professionals who specialize in anxiety.

Generalized Anxiety Disorder

Generalized anxiety disorder (GAD) is diagnosed when a person has experienced uncontrollable anxiety and worry about events and activities as an almost daily occurrence, and the condition has persisted over a six-month period. For a diagnosis of GAD in a teen there must also be at least one physiological symptom, such as rapid heartbeat or excessive sweating. These are young people who worry about the future, their past behavior, their academic and sports abilities and their relationships with other teens. Their parents often describe them as having been worriers since they were little more than babies. Like other anxiety disorders, GAD often co-exists with major depressive disorder.

Worrying about the future is a big problem for teens with GAD. Not only do they worry about things going wrong at school and embarrassing incidents, they also worry about their health, their parents' health, nuclear war and the economy. Teens with GAD tend to expect a great deal of themselves and are exceptionally self-critical about seemingly small things. Rather than being reassuring, successes just seem to make them worry about future failures.

A teen with GAD often needs constant reassurance from parents and teachers. He may think that a teacher has given him a good grade so as not to disappoint him and may not believe evidence to the contrary.

These young people exaggerate the potential consequences of their actions (they might really think their parents won't love them if they come in late); they believe that catastrophes are likely to occur; and they are almost certain that when bad things happen, they will not be able to cope.

As with other anxiety problems, treatment may involve teaching the teen strategies to deal with anxiety, such as ways to mentally reframe tense situations and specific coping skills. Traditional psychotherapy may make the teen feel much worse as she explores how she feels. It can intensify the anxiety without teaching her how to take control.

With treatment, many of these teens improve, although a large number will eventually move into a more narrow category of anxiety problem. Many teens find useful ways to live with anxiety and even put it to good use vocationally. For example, troubleshooting jobs can involve imagining a worst-case scenario and then developing strategies for prevention.

Panic Disorder

A diagnosis of panic disorder will not be made unless the teen has experienced recurrent panic attacks, and has had problems for at least a month after each attack, including such things as worrying excessively about having another attack, worrying about the consequences of the attack or exhibiting a major change in behavior because of it.

Panic attacks are quite common in adolescence. They start abruptly and peak within ten minutes. They are episodes of intense fear and can include a number of symptoms: palpitations or increased heart rate, sweating, shaking and dry mouth. Symptoms often include difficulty breathing, a feeling of choking, chest pain, nausea or abdominal pain. The teen may have chills or feel hot, and may have numbness or tingling in his hands and feet or around his mouth. He may feel dizzy or light-headed and may have a feeling that objects around him aren't real. He may also feel that he "isn't really there." He may have an intense fear of losing control or passing out, and he may be afraid that he is dying.

Actual panic disorder is not common in young teens. It tends to start later in adolescence or young adulthood. Panic disorder can co-exist with depression. In addition, panic attacks are common in depressed teens.

The teen who has occasional panic attacks should be reassured that she won't die, that the attack is always time-limited and that it may disappear without treatment. Panic disorder can be treated with cognitive therapy, SSRIs or clonazepam.

Treatment for Anxiety Disorders

Anxiety disorders in adolescents are often successfully treated. Even after treatment, these teens may not be completely free of anxiety, but for most anxiety no longer interferes in a significant way with their functioning.

The techniques developed by experts in the field of anxiety are not yet routinely used by family doctors and pediatricians. I am sure that in the next few years workshops in these treatments will be taught at many continuing-education events, and primary care physicians will be trained to deal effectively with many anxiety problems in children and adolescents.

Older drugs used for anxiety (anxiolytics) cause drowsiness and problems with coordination. The newer antidepressants, which have fewer side effects and are being used in anxious teens, are especially useful if the teen also has depression. Other drugs in development will be targeted more specifically at anxiety.

If you're a parent with an anxious child, it may feel as if anxiety is a catching condition! It *is* anxiety-provoking for parents to live with an anxious child. Try to look ahead to a time when your teen will have had successful treatment and will be happy and able to reach her potential. If you can picture this, it will calm you, and this calmness might help your teen.

9. Medical Conditions and Depression

This chapter will explore the links to depression that may be found in a number of medical conditions occurring in adolescence. We will also look at the possible connections between illness and depressed mood.

Some Medical Conditions Can Look Like Depression ...

Josh was a 17-year-old who was practically dragged to our clinic by his father, Dan. Josh was a bit concerned that he wasn't doing well at school, but said things were otherwise fine. Dan was worried that Josh was severely depressed. "He picks at his food. After school he wraps an afghan around himself and settles in on the couch watching TV. He never sees his friends. His grades have plummeted, and his teachers say he doesn't seem to be able to concentrate. He says he's not depressed, but he seems sad and lethargic to me. He goes to bed early, and we have to drag him out of bed in the morning."

The afghan was the tipoff. It had been a warm spring, and we wondered why Josh was feeling cold when everyone else was warm. On further questioning, we discovered that Josh had gained ten pounds during the time his father said he was barely eating. A physical examination and lab tests confirmed that Josh's thyroid gland was underactive (hypothyroidism). He had met enough criteria for a clinical depression, but all his symptoms were caused by a low level of thyroid hormone. Six weeks after he started treatment for thyroid problems, Josh's school performance had improved, and his father said he was back to his old self.

A high level of thyroid hormone (hyperthyroidism) could have also mimicked a depression. In that case, Josh would have been losing weight, perhaps seeming agitated and having difficulty concentrating. He might have had trouble falling asleep or staying asleep. We would wonder about hyperthyroidism if he was eating more than usual but still losing weight, and if he felt hotter than other people in the family.

Another patient of mine, Cathy, complained that she felt tired all the time. She fell asleep easily at night and had a hard time getting up in the morning. This didn't surprise me. She was an A student at an academically challenging school, was on a local soccer team and played the violin. She reported that she felt down, and that her friends said she wasn't as much fun, although she still enjoyed many of her activities. She had heavy periods and was a vegetarian, so I wondered if what looked like a depression might actually be anemia. She didn't have any physical complaints to make me suspect anything else. When I checked her blood, I found that Cathy *was* anemic, but she also had a high erythrocyte sedimentation rate, a test that indicates inflammation somewhere in the body. Shortly after, she developed symptoms of inflammatory bowel disease (IBD).

Many illnesses such as Crohn's disease, ulcerative colitis, hepatitis and lupus can present with some of the symptoms of depression. It is important to recognize that teen problems are not always psychological, and to check for other medical conditions.

... and Some Medical Conditions Can Lead to Depression

Many chronic medical problems start in childhood or adolescence. About 4 percent of teens have a condition that limits their activities or causes them to miss significant time at school because of illness or doctors' appointments. It would be hard to pick out most of these young people by sight. Few are in wheelchairs or have an obvious disability. Many are severe asthmatics, suffer from migraines, have seizure disorders or any of a number of rarer conditions.

It is easy to see that it could be stressful for these teens to feel different from their peers, to be limited at times because of a condition, and perhaps to be treated differently by parents. These experiences certainly could cause teens with disabling conditions to become depressed, but most do not, although they may go through periods of sadness, grief or despair because of the limitations caused by the illness, cultural perceptions of illness, or other issues. Teens with disabling conditions may be better at seeking help than other adolescents because they know who to ask for help and feel that it is acceptable to do so, and therefore get help before they sink into a diagnosable depression.

Some studies have shown that disabled and non-disabled

people have similar levels of depression, while other studies have shown that disabled people have higher levels of depression. One of these studies showed less of a gender difference between disabled men and women than between men and women without disabilities.

Teens with chronic illness or disability who are at higher risk of depression seem to be those whose medication can cause depression, those with some neurological problems and those with poor social supports. Protective factors include good family support, low maternal anxiety and less severe forms of an illness.

Psychological factors can adversely affect a medical condition, such as when hopelessness causes a relapse or delays recovery, or when anxiety about side effects leads to missed medication doses.

Specific Illnesses

HIV/AIDS

AIDS (acquired immune deficiency syndrome) is still a fairly uncommon disease in teens. Because there is a long lag time between becoming infected with HIV and developing AIDS, most people who are infected as adolescents do not become ill until they are in their twenties, and for many of these young people, their HIV-positive status is not even identified until they get sick. However, by the time they are teens, those infected as fetuses or babies have often had to deal with the major life issues of having a parent or parents who are sick with AIDS or who have died from the illness.

AIDS is a disease that primarily affects the body's ability

to fight infection. People with AIDS can get sick from germs that don't usually make people ill, or that cause only minor illness in someone who is otherwise healthy. People with AIDS may get infections in body parts that are normally protected. They are also more susceptible to certain types of cancer. As well, there are symptoms that go with AIDS that are not directly associated with infections.

It isn't surprising that many HIV-infected people say that they are sad, worried or tense. The majority of people with HIV feel fine physically, but may live in fear of the virus's potentially devastating effects. HIV-infected teens may vacillate between denial and dread, sometimes seeming to forget that they have a problem and at other times noticing the smallest changes in their bodies.

Adults with AIDS who are depressed are more likely to die than their non-depressed peers, perhaps as a direct result of depression or because of disturbances of hormones that can be associated with depression. It could also be that people who are depressed and have AIDS have more difficulty taking their medications correctly, leading to rapid disease progression. They may smoke more, making them more susceptible to pneumonia. They may also use more alcohol and other recreational drugs, further increasing the difficulty of taking their medications and leading to dangerous drug interactions or accidental drug overdoses. Adults with AIDS have been shown to be more likely to kill themselves than people with other terminal illnesses.

It is important that symptoms of depression in someone with AIDS be investigated thoroughly. HIV can invade the brain and cause neurologic problems that mimic depression. Some of the early signs of AIDS dementia include slowed thinking, poor attention and concentration, memory problems and apathy. Some of these symptoms can also be caused by medications (such as antinausea drugs), brain infections or tumors.

You should also be aware that some common problems associated with AIDS, such as poor appetite and sleep disorders, may be caused by depression. Don't assume that these difficulties always arise from the AIDS itself.

Diabetes Mellitus

John is a 15-year-old diabetic who had been having problems at home, both with his parents and his younger brother, for several months. John's parents brought him to the hospital for a psychiatric evaluation because they were worried that he had been depressed for the past month. He was having difficulty falling asleep, was waking up several times during the night and then having a hard time getting up in the morning. His appetite was erratic. His energy was low and he was having problems at school, especially with concentration.

In addition to a psychiatric assessment, John had a number of blood tests. The one that reflects long-term diabetic control showed that John's diabetes management was far from adequate. It was obvious that he had not been taking enough insulin.

When John's diabetes was brought under control, his sleep habits, energy and concentration improved significantly. He no longer appeared depressed, although he was still very unhappy at home and fighting with his brother and parents. He received individual counseling that helped him deal with issues at home and, as things improved, he found it easier to manage his diabetes.

Diabetes is an inability to metabolize sugar properly, a fairly common disease in adolescence. If not treated, it can cause serious, fairly immediate complications. When a teen does not take enough insulin (because of skipped doses, for instance), short-term complications may not be very obvious, but many long-term problems result. If too much insulin is used, blood sugar levels can become very low.

Control of diabetes involves a balance of exercise, food intake and injections of insulin, and it is important to be aware that stress can destabilize this balance.

A depressed diabetic teen may have trouble with this delicate balance of lifestyle and medication. Feelings of helplessness and hopelessness can have a negative effect on her ability to pay attention to controlling her diabetes. Depression interferes with abstract thinking skills and the ability to concentrate, making diabetes therapy, which is largely self-directed, difficult. Decreased levels of activity and food intake can also change insulin needs. A depressed person may not notice the early warning signs of a blood sugar level that is too high or too low.

Migraine

Although many of us think of migraines as an adult phenomenon, children and teens do get migraine headaches.

Migraines are more than just bad headaches. The throbbing pain of a migraine is often severe, and usually focused on one side of the head. Untreated, a migraine can last from four hours to three days. In addition to headache, migraines often include sensitivity to light (photophobia) or sound (phonophobia), nausea and vomiting.

Ten to 20 percent of migraine sufferers experience what is called an aura, which usually comes just before an attack. It may involve visual problems like flashing vision, zigzag lines or visual holes; or there may be disturbances in the sense of touch, smell and hearing.

There is research that links migraine to depression (and

also to anxiety). Adults with migraines are up to four times as likely to have major depression as those who don't. Also, people with depression or anxiety are more likely to have migraines. This research indicates that depression is often a later phenomenon in migraine, occurring in adulthood. Of course, many teens with migraines do not have depression.

Depression occurring with migraine tends to be associated with irritability, fatigue, lack of energy and weight gain. However, these conditions sometimes occur as side effects of medications used to prevent migraines, so it is important to consider this possibility in a teen who seems depressed and is on medication.

The fact that specific symptoms are associated with migraine and depression makes me wonder if this is a separate syndrome, distinct from other types of depression. It is possible that there is a common, neurotransmitter-mediated cause for both the headaches and the depression. Migraine and depression occurring together may have a genetic component, as the combination seems to run in families.

Migraines can be triggered by stress, inadequate sleep, skipping meals, certain foods and certain times in the menstrual cycle. A teen might be motivated to try to stay on top of these factors, but parents cannot expect an adolescent to avoid all triggers in all situations, as she may make choices for social, academic or developmental reasons that supersede migraine prevention.

Some antidepressants also help prevent migraines and can be used to treat a depression with this advantageous "side effect." People with bipolar disorder and migraine can use the seizure medication valproate to prevent migraines.

There is no evidence that preventing migraines changes the incidence of depression.

Lupus

Teens can get a variety of diseases in the arthritis category. One of these diseases is systemic lupus erythematosus, known as lupus or SLE.

Many parts of the body can be attacked when a teen has lupus, including the skin, joints, kidneys and brain. Some teens with lupus have many prolonged hospitalizations, while others respond well to treatment and do not need this intensive help. Lupus is a disease that can come and go, so a teen may have long periods of time when she is well, punctuated by flare-ups when she must restart or increase her medications. Girls are more likely to get lupus, although it is not exclusively a female disease. No direct links have been shown between lupus or arthritis and depression.

Body image and self-esteem issues can be important for teens with lupus. There can be major body changes as a result of steroid treatment, including slow growth, weight gain and acne. In addition, teens with lupus may have a noticeable rash on the face. None of these things alone will cause a major depression, but they can certainly lead to sadness or distress, which could contribute to the development of a depression.

People with lupus are very sensitive to the sun and can get sick even with moderate exposure. Although potent sunscreens help, teens with this condition also have to cover up. They may feel self-conscious about going out with long sleeves and a hat and stay inside instead, thus missing out on social contact. This situation could also lead to some distress.

Although these teens are as likely to get depressed as other teens, it is important for a depressed teen with lupus to be checked out by her doctor. Major depressive disorder can be an early sign that there is brain involvement with the lupus (CNS lupus), which is something that should be aggressively treated.

Cystic Fibrosis

Cystic fibrosis is an inherited disease that has a major effect on the lungs and the gastrointestinal tract of the sufferer. Most people with cystic fibrosis are diagnosed early in life. The range of severity is quite wide, with some teens having almost no hospital admissions and others practically living in the hospital. Despite the disease's high mortality rate and a fairly demanding treatment schedule, most teens with cystic fibrosis are well adjusted and do not seem to be any more likely than other teens to become depressed.

A big issue for these young people is that their physical development tends to be late. They may find it upsetting that health care workers, teachers, parents and even friends treat them as if they were younger than they are, just because they are smaller and not as developed physically. However, this does not usually lead to a depression.

Genetic Disorders

Genes are bits of information stored in chromosomes in body cells. Because of a huge amount of information duplication, miscoding of genes does not often cause a problem. When it does, malfunctions can occur in any system of the body. Genetic disorders, such as Down syndrome, often involve more than one system. Some genetic conditions are associated with a "different" appearance, so the teen's self-esteem and body image can be affected; some disorders are associated with decreased intelligence, and this may also be a cause of distress—teens can be very sensitive to the perceptions that others have of them or of any decreased capabilities they may have. Discrimination, put-downs and feeling different can clearly have a negative effect on mood.

There are specific links between certain genetic disorders and depression. A syndrome called velo-cardiac-facial syndrome is strongly associated with bipolar disorder. About two-thirds of people with the syndrome have diagnosable bipolar disorder by adulthood, most presenting in late childhood or early adolescence.

Chronic Fatigue Syndrome (CFS) and Fibromyalgia (FM)

Chronic fatigue syndrome and fibromyalgia are similar illnesses with overlapping symptoms. A striking feature of both is long-term, debilitating fatigue. Teens with these conditions may experience fever, weight loss, sore throat, headaches, difficulty thinking and sleep difficulties. Fibromyalgia also involves severe muscle aches.

Parents often report that their teens look terrible on bad days—"pale" and "drained" being common words used to describe them. It is important to have other diseases such as inflammatory bowel disease and hypothyroidism ruled out before a diagnosis of either CFS or FM is made. Teens with these conditions seem to have a much better chance of recovery than adults, and they recover more quickly.

Both CFS and FM are associated with mood swings. Because so many of the symptoms are the same as depression, it can be hard to tell whether a teen with one of these problems is depressed. When a depression is treated, some symptoms that have been attributed to CFS or FM may clear up. Many, but not all, teens with these problems have pre-existing psychological problems, including depression.

Some doctors think that CFS and FM are just depression variants, and that these conditions don't really exist as separately diagnosable illnesses. However, some symptoms cannot be explained by depression. One theory about these conditions is that teen sufferers have disturbances in their immune system that are a result of stress or psychological problems. A viral illness then triggers an abnormal immune response. Another theory (the two theories are not necessarily mutually exclusive) is that these illnesses are serotonin-mediated, like depression. If so, treatments with antidepressants may be helpful for many of the symptoms, and not just for depression, sleep problems or mood swings.

Seizure Disorders (Epilepsy)

Seizures are caused by abnormal bursts of energy within the brain. Although many people think all seizures are grand mal seizures, with major movements and changes in level of consciousness, there are other kinds, and teens as well as adults experience them. Some teens have frequent seizures, during which they become unaware of their surroundings for a few seconds. Teachers may think that those adolescents are daydreaming. Other teens have motor seizures that affect only a small part of the body.

Teens with seizure disorders often want to hide their condition from their friends, and live in fear that they will have a grand mal seizure in class or at the mall.

Few references in the literature link depression and seizure disorders, and the experts I talked with were unaware of any connection. Theoretically, teens with seizure disorders should actually experience a lower rate of depression. Since induced seizures (through electroconvulsive therapy, see Chapter 6) are used to treat severe depression, one would expect that naturally occuring seizures would also have a positive effect.

To control their seizures, many sufferers take carbamazepine or valproic acid, both of which have also been used to treat bipolar depression.

Inflammatory Bowel Disease (IBD): Ulcerative colitis and Crohn's Disease

Ulcerative colitis and Crohn's disease are inflammatory bowel diseases that affect children, teens and adults. About a quarter of the people with these diseases get them before adulthood. They are chronic conditions that can become unexpectedly better or worse. Many teens with these diseases experience diarrhea, rectal bleeding, weight loss and abdominal pain. The onset of puberty can be late for teens with IBD, and they may have problems with growth, especially if they have Crohn's disease.

Some symptoms of these diseases, and some of the side effects of medications used for them, are similar to depression symptoms. Low energy, fatigue, sleep problems and appetite and weight changes may all occur with both depression and IBD, making it somewhat more difficult to diagnose depression.

A number of studies have shown that teens with IBD seem to be more psychologically vulnerable than teens with other illnesses. Some studies have shown rates of depression ranging from 20 to 40 percent. The teens in one study reported social isolation, loneliness and shame, all of which could predispose them to depression. However, these studies used standard scales for depression that include symptoms that could also be attributed to IBD.

Parents of teens with IBD should be aware that stressful life events may precipitate a depression, especially in a teen who is having social problems related to his perception of the disease. These teens might benefit from an opportunity to talk honestly with other adolescents with IBD, through a support group or Internet contact.

Thyroid Disease

The thyroid gland controls the rate at which the body works. The gland responds to hormones made by the pituitary gland, which in turn is controlled by a part of the brain called the hypothalamus. There are a number of causes for imbalances in the level of thyroid hormone made by this gland. Some are autoimmune disorders (in which the immune system, instead of protecting the body, attacks it), inflammation, problems with the brain hormones that control the gland and (rarely) malignancies.

Both too much thyroid hormone (hyperthyroidism) and too little (hypothyroidism) can look very much like depression.

The teen who is hypothyroid lacks energy and may have poor concentration and difficulty thinking. She may feel down, sleep a lot and have a decreased appetite. Despite eating less, she gains weight (unlike depression, where teens with decreased appetite tend to lose weight). Signs of hypothyroidism that are different from depression are dry skin and hair and an intolerance of cold. All the symptoms go away with treatment.

Teens who are hyperthyroid feel agitated. Although they initially feel quite energized, they may end up feeling tired. They also can have difficulty concentrating and difficulty falling or staying asleep. They eat more but lose weight. They cannot tolerate heat. Hyperthyroidism is less likely to be confused with depression than hypothyroidism even though many of its signs are found in depressed teens. Parents are more likely to think that a teen with this condition is taking drugs.

Multiple Sclerosis (MS)

Multiple sclerosis affects the ability of the brain and the spinal cord to conduct electrical impulses because of damage to the coating on the nerves. Although MS is much more common in adults, it can occur in teens.

Multiple sclerosis can start with many different symptoms, depending on what part of the nervous system is attacked. Often there is only one symptom at first, which can be weakness, numbness, clumsiness or visual problems. Since it is a disease that can come and go, a teen who is in remission may be fearful of a recurrence. MS can be difficult to diagnose in a teen, and repeated testing, visits to specialists and uncertainty about the cause of the problem can all lead to feelings of depression.

Mood swings, apathy, difficulty concentrating and depression have all been described in MS, and if one of these is the only symptom in the initial stage of the disease, depression or other psychiatric problems might be diagnosed instead of MS.

Head Injury

Many people have noted that depression can follow a head injury. Considering that brain trauma can alter almost every aspect of a teen's life, including academic abilities, memory, personality, control over impulses and ability to move, it isn't surprising that many young people become depressed a year or two into their rehabilitation, when the full impact of their condition starts to sink in. In some ways, this depression is really a grief reaction. However, teens in general do better after a brain injury than adults in areas such as vocation, social relationships and physical abilities.

However, some brain-injured teens become depressed much sooner than this, and in others the depression persists far longer than one would expect from grief. Some of these teens may be suffering from depression that is a direct result of the trauma. This is perhaps related to the site of the trauma, the type of injury or a predisposition to depression.

Studies examining depression after head trauma show widely varying results, giving rates as low as 10 percent and as high as 75 percent. It isn't surprising, then, that the diagnosis of depression is complicated in the brain-injured teen. Physical symptoms, like sleep problems and appetite and weight changes, are common after head trauma and are not helpful in distinguishing which of these teens have a major depressive disorder. In addition, after a head injury some teens experience a state of extremely heightened awareness of physical feelings and of their environment. Mildly depressed mood may be translated into full-blown depression; small daily aches and pains may be viewed as major physical problems. This extra-sensitive reaction to the internal and external environment can lead to overdiagnosis of depression. The high rate of sleep difficulties after head injuries, leading to depressed mood, irritability and lack of energy, may also be misdiagnosed as depression.

A history of substance use often accounts for head injuries —many of these head injuries are alcohol related, including motor vehicle accidents and diving accidents. After the injury, substance abuse problems may continue or worsen. Substance use can make a depression worse or mask a depression.

Depression in a teen with a head injury must be treated. Because many antidepressants lower the threshold for seizures, and because seizures are a common complication of head injuries, medication needs to be prescribed with caution, in the lowest possible doses and well monitored.

Remember, Depression Should Always Be Treated

Parents should never assume that depression is "just part of the illness" in a teen with a chronic condition. We might be tempted to think, "I'd be depressed too if I had to take all those medications or miss so many activities," but a major depressive disorder is not usually a part of another chronic illness. Depression may be a sign that the illness is worsening and needs special investigation or treatment (as with CNS lupus) or may be unrelated to the disease. These teens should not have to put up with being depressed when treatments are available.

10. Special Cases

There are children who, in various ways, are different from their peers, and as we have seen, difference can be associated with depression. By the time they reach their teen years, some of these kids will be depressed. Some special cases are teens who are very smart. Others are teens with psychiatric diagnoses. In general, when depression exists with another psychiatric diagnosis, the depression is more severe, lasts longer, is harder to treat, is more likely to return once treated and is more likely to result in suicide.

You may be reluctant to look for depression in a son or daughter who has another diagnosis. You may feel that you have more than enough to deal with already. You may be making an effort to see your child in a more "normal" light. But because depression is treatable, it is important to identify it. Doctors may focus only on the diagnosed problem, and if a specialist doesn't know your child well, he may think that signs of depression are just part of your teen's personality. If your teen is depressed, you may find that problems that were thought to be caused by the other psychiatric problem actually improve when your child's depression is treated.

The Very Smart Teen

I don't like the term *gifted*, as I think all children have gifts. To imply that high intelligence is the only gift devalues social, artistic and athletic talents. It encourages a system that segregates smart children from their peers, and both groups then lose the opportunity to learn from each other.

Higher-than-average intelligence actually provides some protection against depression, but there are certainly many smart kids who get depressed. Depression can be harder to detect in a teen who spends a lot of time thinking, brooding on the world's problems or reading the works of pessimistic philosophers. Separating what they are actually feeling from thoughts about depressing topics can be hard. For the smart teen who is also a loner, the usual social markers of depression may just be a reflection of his usual lifestyle.

Treatment Issues

Therapy can also be difficult with a teen who focuses on thinking and being articulate. He may seem more interested in playing word games than in talking about his feelings. He may have read psychology books and may feel that he should be able to keep a step ahead of a therapist. A therapist who is insecure about her own intelligence may feel competitive with the teen. Therapy will not be successful in these circumstances. Staff associated with special programs for teens with higher-than-average intelligence may know about therapists who are good with this group.

A teen who has been told over and over that she is "special" and different might resist taking medication for depression, believing that these drugs are for "ordinary" people. She is more likely than other teens to read everything she can about the drug and see any changes in her body as a side effect.

Learning Disabilities

Learning disabilities (LD) encompass a broad range of problems that include difficulties with taking in and processing information (heard, seen or felt), integrating that information and creating output based on it—in other words, acting in response to the input by speaking, writing or doing. These disabilities can be so mild that they go unnoticed (in which case the term "disability" doesn't really apply) or so severe that they prevent any academic achievement without major intervention. It is important to note that learning disabilities are not related to intelligence.

Some children with learning disabilities go undiagnosed until Grades 7 or 8, when it becomes harder to "fake it." The level of work becomes more abstract, and simple memorization cannot pull them through anymore. Ironically, the intimate school setting of the child's earlier years may prevent identification of learning disabilities, as the teacher says to herself, "His spelling is so poor because he's thinking so fast," or "She's so busy socializing that she doesn't concentrate on her work." In middle school, students rotate through classes, and teachers have large numbers of students to evaluate. Teachers count on test results and grades on assignments for these evaluations and are less likely to take into account other circumstances when assessing the child. When the student then does badly on her report card, the parents may demand an explanation, which can lead to testing and identification of the problem.

A depression that starts at this age can mimic a learning

problem. A teen may turn in work that is incomplete or sloppy, skip school or be inattentive in class, and in general exhibit a seeming lack of concern about the future or about not performing up to expectations.

It makes sense that a teen with an undiagnosed learning disability who has experienced significant academic difficulty, would feel powerless and helpless and therefore be prone to depression, especially if she is unlucky enough to have a biological predisposition to this problem. The resulting depression can then compound the problem by negatively affecting the teen's academic achievement, perhaps resulting in feelings of shame and more helplessness, deepening the depression. It is therefore important to diagnose depression in a teen with a learning disorder so as to stop this vicious cycle.

When a depression and learning disability occur together, it can make it more difficult to come up with an accurate diagnosis. Moreover, a teen with a learning problem may have difficulty completing some of the standardized tests used to help diagnose psychological problems.

Having both depression and a learning disability increases the risk of dropping out of school, having trouble with finding jobs in later adolescence and having poor coping skills. A depressed teen with LD might have problems seeking out academic help, responding to new learning strategies or being flexible in his approach to learning.

Teens with learning disabilities may be more prone to depression than those without, although studies looking at the connections between them have had conflicting results. Low self-esteem is often a hallmark of the teen with learning problems, compounded by problems knowing how to relate to others. However, not everyone with low self-esteem becomes depressed.

A study that compared Grade 5 and 6 students with and without learning disabilities showed that in both groups, children who were depressed rated themselves lower in athletic skills and in their perceptions of their behavior, but only the depressed LD children gave themselves low ratings for social acceptance. This is probably not just a subjective feeling. Some studies have shown lower rates of acceptance by peers for children with learning problems.

A study of older teens and adults with learning problems showed that people with LD were much less likely to identify depression in themselves than other people in their lives were. Interestingly, the people with learning problems were more likely to identify panic disorders and phobias in themselves.

In a family where one or more children have a learning disability, levels of stress may be high. Parents are likely to be expending large amounts of energy fighting for appropriate resources; they may also have to deal with competitive extended family members who like to think that their kids are smarter and, often, with their own feelings of parental guilt. These high stress levels could be a factor in a teen's depression, in behavior problems for both the LD and other children, and in marital conflict.

Children and teens with learning disabilities and poor social skills seem more likely to become depressed than those with average or good social skills. The majority of teens with learning disabilities have some problems with social competence. This could be part of whatever underlying neurological problem has led to the learning problem. Adolescents with learning disabilities may have been placed in special classes where their limited opportunities to interact with non-disabled peers are curtailed. These teens' feelings of resentment or unhappiness about being separated from "normal" peers may be linked with depression, decreased social skills, and lower self-esteem.

Students with learning disabilities report difficulties with non-verbal communication and with social problem solving. As these problems can affect them academically, isolate them socially and color their view of the world, it may be hard to determine which came first—the poor social skills or the depression. A further complicating factor is that some teens with LD may have poor social skills related to attention deficit hyperactivity disorder (ADHD), rather than from factors associated with their learning difficulties.

Many proposals have been put forward to classify learning disabilities. Parents of a sizable number of children have been told that their children have a learning disability, when in fact there are other reasons for their poor school performance. A classification system would be helpful, because it does seem that teens with specific types of learning problems are at higher risk for depression.

Teens with learning disabilities seem to have a higher risk of suicide than teens without these disabilities. There could be a number of reasons for this. Higher rates of depression in this group would lead to higher rates of suicide. The poor social skills of LD teens might lead to their being bullied, which can be a catalyst for a suicide attempt. A teen with a learning disability might lack thinking skills that would help him figure out a less lethal solution to his problems.

Treatment Issues

When you're looking for a therapist, it is important to find one whose approach matches your teen's learning style. For instance, a therapist who relies on talking only could be a bad therapeutic fit for a teen with an auditory processing or language problem. A teen with a visual-motor deficit might do better with a talk therapist than an art therapist. The therapist should be able to demonstrate some knowledge of LD so that you and your teen don't have to spend a lot of time educating this person.

Your local learning disabilities association might have a list of therapists who are experienced in working with these teens.

Attention Deficit Hyperactivity Disorder (ADHD)

Many children and teens are being diagnosed with attention deficit hyperactivity disorder. Some of them probably warrant this diagnosis, while others are difficult kids who are being "fixed" with stimulant medication. In the past, those with a mild form of the disorder probably wouldn't have been treated or even diagnosed. Studies tend to be done on more severely affected young people, and their findings probably do not apply to the entire spectrum of ADHD.

ADHD is usually defined by the behaviors that accompany it—not the inattentiveness and impulsivity themselves, but the fidgeting, running around, school failure, loud talking and sleep problems that accompany what is going on internally.

Children with ADHD have a high incidence of anxiety disorders, but teens with ADHD do not show this strong association. The evidence about depression and ADHD is less clear; some studies identify levels of depression in ADHD children that are similar to levels in the general population, and other research shows an overwhelming majority of such children and teens with depression or another mood disorder. When these are all put together, it appears that close to half of all children with ADHD will have a mood disorder at some time in their lives. One definite finding is that if there is a gene for ADHD, it isn't linked to the gene for bipolar disorder, as children with ADHD have only the normal risk of developing manic depression.

Most teens with ADHD experience academic problems, which may be a direct result of the ADHD, but about a quarter of these young people also have learning disabilities. The fact that people in both groups are at risk for depression means that, presumably, the risk is even higher if they have both.

Teens with ADHD tend to be quite impulsive. Low levels of impulsivity are associated with resilience, the ability to do well despite stress and life problems, so any programs that help teens learn to stop and think before acting should help prevent depression.

ADHD is often treated with stimulant medication. Some of the side effects of these medications are the same as symptoms experienced by depressed teens—insomnia, agitation and loss of appetite. Teens who are on both stimulants and antidepressants need to be monitored closely.

Treatment Issues

Teens with ADHD have usually already received intensive academic, medical and psychological intervention and may resist getting treatment for depression. Moreover, their siblings (and parents) may resent another time-consuming treatment.

Doctors treating the depression should be aware of any potential interactions between stimulant medication and the antidepressants they prescribe. Antidepressants that can cause agitation should be avoided.

Therapists who are inexperienced with ADHD can find these teens very frustrating and difficult. Therapy that requires the patient to sit quietly and have long conversations will not suit most of these teens.

A local ADHD parent support group or association may be able to provide names of doctors and therapists who work with these teens.

Eating Disorders

Anorexia nervosa and depression are illnesses that can be confused in adolescence. The depressed teen who has lost her appetite and is losing weight may be thought to have an eating disorder. As many teens without eating disorders are unhappy with their body size and shape and would like to lose weight, an in-depth assessment is often needed to tease out the real diagnosis.

Conversely, the teen with anorexia nervosa may experience an inability to concentrate, sleep disturbance, feelings of sadness and irritability as a result of the food deprivation that is part of the illness. If this is the case, the symptoms improve when the teen regains the lost weight.

Eating disorders can also co-exist with depression. Studies have shown that anywhere from 20 to 90 percent of people with anorexia nervosa are depressed. With the confusion that can be created by the similarity of symptoms, I think that 90 percent is higher than the actual rate. Similar rates of depression have been found in people with bulimia nervosa, a syndrome in which binge eating is followed by vomiting, purging or fasting. There is some evidence that depression and bulimia may be genetically linked, which is not the case for anorexia nervosa. At least one study of women who had attempted suicide (compared with a group of women who came to an emergency department with minor accidental injuries) showed a significantly higher incidence of bulimia nervosa in the suicidal women.

Bulimia and seasonal affective disorder can be found together—it could be argued that they are related diseases. They share some of the same symptoms (overeating, carbohydrate craving and weight gain). There is some evidence that bulimia becomes more severe in the winter, and some people have tried treating bulimia with light therapy. In many of these patients, the depression appears to predate the eating disorder.

Eating disorders can also coexist with other psychiatric problems. Perhaps the most common is obsessive-compulsive disorder, a kind of anxiety disorder.

A number of studies have looked at the treatment of bulimia nervosa and coexisting depression. Most have shown an improvement in both depression and bulimic symptoms with SSRI treatment.

Treatment Issues

Practically speaking, if your teen has been diagnosed with depression and decreased dietary intake and weight loss are part of it, you should see an improvement as her depression gets better. If you don't, ask her how she is feeling about her body and whether she is happy with her weight. Notice whether she seems to be avoiding high-fat or high-calorie foods, or if she is avoiding mealtime altogether. Talk to her doctor about the possibility that she has an eating disorder.

On the other hand, if your teen has anorexia or bulimia and continues to show poor concentration, a low mood or other signs of depression even as her medical condition is stabilized and she is gaining weight, it might be that she is depressed. Don't expect antidepressants to cure the eating disorder.

Programs for teens with eating disorders usually include a psychiatrist as part of the team. In addition to treating the eating disorder, the psychiatrist will look for depression in these young people and should be willing to discuss the possibility of depression with the teen and her parents.

Many cities have support groups for teens with eating disorders and for their parents; a group of this type may be able to suggest a doctor with an interest in both eating disorders and depression.

Teens with eating disorders might resist medication, thinking that it is a trick to make them take something that will make them fat. Just as they hide or throw away food, they might also dispose of medications and so should be watched closely.

Sleep Problems

A teen patient told me that "The worst thing about being depressed is how badly I sleep. I lie in bed at night and I just can't seem to drop off. I can hardly drag myself out of bed in the morning. I feel that if I could just get some sleep, I would feel a lot better." She asked me to prescribe sleeping pills because she was sure they would help.

Sleeping pills are not a good idea for teens. They will help sufferers sleep for a while, but eventually they stop working and the teen's problems are worse than ever. On the other hand, many teens on antidepressants find that they sleep better.

A teen who feels depressed and is having sleep problems may not actually have a major depression. Lack of energy, poor concentration and low spirits can be a result of sleeping badly. If sleep problems started before any signs of depression, it might be worthwhile to explore other causes of the sleep difficulty.

Teens who have problems sleeping should consider either cutting out all caffeine, as it is a stimulant, or restricting intake to the morning, so the effect can wear off before bedtime. Caffeine is an ingredient in many soft drinks as well as in chocolate, coffee and tea.

Teens who are under a lot of stress may also have trouble sleeping. They might not be worrying about anything in particular, but they feel revved up at bedtime. Is there something specific your teen is worrying about? Thinking about problems with friends, past sexual abuse, school issues or other difficulties can keep her awake at night, with the thoughts going round and round in her head like an endless tape.

Poor "sleep hygiene" can also lead to difficulties falling asleep. Good sleep hygiene includes using the bed only for sleep (no TV in the bedroom!), having a bedtime routine, and getting exercise during the day. Some teens find that it helps to take a warm bath about half an hour before going to bed.

When the body's natural clock gets reset to a sleep time that is not compatible with a teen's schedule, many problems ensue. We call this a sleep cycle disorder. Young people with this problem often fall asleep at three or four in the morning, but then have to get up in time to go to school. The new sleep cycle becomes even more entrenched if the teen comes home from school and has a nap. Sleep cycle disturbances are corrected by setting bedtime ahead by half an hour a night until the teen is finally going to bed at the right time. You shouldn't really attempt to make this adjustment on your own, so if you think this may be your teen's problem, get a doctor's advice.

Treatment Issues

Not many sleep disorder clinics are geared to teens, and good ones may have long waiting lists. Some pediatricians and family doctors have experience with these problems.

Diagnosis can be difficult when a sleep disorder and depression coexist. The doctor might need to treat either the depression or the sleep disorder first, and wait to see if the other problem improves too.

Personality Disorders

The disorders that make up this large group of problems are thought to have their roots in early childhood. As the name implies, these disorders exist when personality traits lead to major problems and distress.

Personality disorders are grouped into three general categories. The first group includes paranoid, schizoid and schizotypal personality disorders, and are not commonly diagnosed in teens. The second group includes antisocial, borderline, histrionic and narcissistic disorders. In the third group are those associated with fearful, anxious or dependent behavior.

Of these, borderline personality disorder (so named because it was thought that these patients were on the borderline between neurosis and psychosis) is most likely to be associated with depression. Teens with this problem often worry that they will be abandoned. They tend to have a very childish experience of their feelings and emotional needs, as well as difficulty in appropriately expressing them. They are often very uncertain about major life issues, such as who they are, what they want to do in life, who they are attracted to or what they believe. Their relationships are intense but not stable. They experience frequent mood swings.

Depression in people with borderline personality disorders is more difficult to treat, lasts longer and recurs more frequently than depression in people without personality disorders. People with this problem are likely to try to harm themselves with self-mutilating behavior, such as burning or cutting themselves. There is a high risk of suicide in this group. Because of this risk, antidepressant therapy should not involve medications that are lethal when taken in overdose. All medications should be prescribed and dispensed in small amounts.

Teens with bipolar disorder, especially without mania, may be misdiagnosed as having a borderline personality disorder. Some studies show that people with personality disorders do not seem to be any more likely than the general population to develop bipolar disorder, whereas other studies indicate an increased risk.

Treatment Issues

At the present time, most personality disorders are difficult to treat. At least one study showed that adults with borderline personality disorder who were not depressed improved significantly when treated with an SSRI. As people with borderline personality disorders are known to be "difficult" patients, both because of our lack of success in treatment and also because of various personality characteristics, some therapists avoid caring for them. These teens may miss appointments or change doctors frequently, so it's difficult to provide medication for them on a consistent basis. They may hoard medication for a suicide attempt.

Parents can help by encouraging the teen to stick with the

therapist. They should supervise antidepressant use and make sure the teen is getting to appointments for medication renewal.

Conduct Disorder

Conduct disorder is a common behavior disorder in adolescents. These teens have persistent behavior problems that involve breaking laws or other rules. Many of these teens tell us that they tortured animals or set fires as younger children. As young teens, they often stay out late or even all night, regardless of family rules. They are frequently involved in law-breaking that involves physically harming other people, damaging property, theft or sexual assault.

Teens with conduct disorder often associate with other young people who exhibit antisocial behavior. They have a hard time making friends, and their peer relationships are often typified by bullying or extortion. Many teens with conduct disorder will show great improvements in their behavior as adults, although some go on to have antisocial personality disorder, a similar adult disorder.

Because these teens display little empathy and seem to lack feelings of guilt, it is hard to imagine them being depressed. Their feelings often seem to be angry and aggressive and they blame various predicaments on others, instead of taking personal responsibility. Because depression is more passive and internal than a conduct disorder, it is hard to see the two coexisting—but they do. In fact, researchers have shown that from 10 to 35 percent of teens with a major depressive disorder also have a conduct disorder, although less than 10 percent of all teens have a conduct disorder. Teens with conduct disorder are more likely both to attempt and to complete suicide.

There could be underlying psychobiological causes that are common to both conduct disorder and depression. Some studies have shown that low levels of serotonin activity are associated with impulsivity and aggression. Decreased levels of the same neurotransmitters associated with depression have also been linked to aggressive and impulsive behavior.

Teens with conduct disorder certainly have reasons to feel sad. They tend to do badly in school, are more likely to have been abused or harshly punished than their peers and don't make friends easily. It may also be that some of these teens turn their (very evident) anger both outwards and inwards, resulting in both behavior problems and depression. It could also be that a teen trying to deal with a major depression copes by "acting out" in aggressive ways.

Treatment Issues

You may be able to find specialized programs in mental health facilities or agencies to help your teen with her conduct disorder. Sometimes, teens end up in these programs as a result of a court conviction. You may be looking for residential treatment by this time, both because your teen needs intensive help and because living with a teen who lies, steals and maybe hurts other people is creating unbearable levels of stress for your family. Staff who run outpatient and residential programs may not have much understanding of depression, and might think the teen is "drug-seeking" if he asks for medication. Your family doctor or pediatrician may be able to intervene and provide treatment for the depression.

Grief

A 13-year-old boy was brought to our hospital complaining of
severe chest pain. He was worried that he was having a heart
attack. He had recently had a blood test for high cholesterol, as
his father had died of a heart attack the year before. Julian had
something called chest wall syndrome, a common problem in
young people, caused by spasms in the tiny muscles between the
ribs. Teens with this problem often are feeling stressed or
anxious. Julian's anxiety had been precipitated by the blood test,
but he'd also become stuck in the grief process because he felt
that boys shouldn't cry or talk about their feelings. He put a lot
of energy into taking care of his mother and little sister. Although
his chest pain continued to occur over a number of years, it did
not cause the same level of worry for him after he became
involved with a group of teens who had all lost a parent.

Loss often makes people feel sad, angry, guilty and helpless.
Grief is an emotional process that results from large losses. We
think of grief as being related to death, but it is also experienced when we or loved ones lose our health; become disabled; or lose a job, home, relationship or religious conviction.

Grief is a normal process, and although the person experiencing it may feel depressed and experience the physical
symptoms of depression, it becomes depression only when
the griever is stuck in the process. Grief can be felt in anticipation of a loss, such as when a parent, friend or relative is
dying, or when parents are in the process of splitting up. If
a teen allows herself to experience this grief, rather than

denying the feelings, she is more likely to be able to move through the process without becoming depressed. It is an experience that may allow the teen to express feelings, to regroup and to eventually find meaning in life. Despite the teen's feelings that no one else could possibly understand how she is feeling, grieving often mobilizes support from friends.

Symptoms that accompany grief overlap with the symptoms of depression. Teens may be unable to sleep or sleep more than usual; have headaches or stomachaches; experience loss of appetite, increased eating and a tight feeling in the throat. Although crying is often a major feature of grief, not all teens cry during this time. Adolescents who are grieving often experience lack of concentration, disorganization, anger, difficulties at work or school, feeling "like a robot" and fear for their own survival. They may not show outward signs of grief; they may even seem uncaring, but they are almost certainly concealing their feelings. This may come from a concern about "falling apart publicly," a need for privacy, a desire to have friends see them as unchanged or an attempt to deny their emotions. A teen may be able to grieve only for short periods of time, taking comfort in normal life activities in between. Adolescents sometimes experience symptoms similar to those of the person who has died, going to an emergency room or doctor with chest pains, headaches or stomach pains.

Getting Help

Many states and provinces have family bereavement associations with local chapters. They often provide group and individual help for bereaved teens.

A bereavement counselor may suggest a psychiatrist who

has an interest in bereavement for a teen who appears to be depressed as well as grieving. Teens should be told that the goal of this therapy is to help with their depression, not to make the grief go away. Grieving teens may fear that the treatment will make them forget the person who died, or try to make them feel happy about the death. They need to be reassured that no one intends an outcome like that.

11. Adolescent Suicide

When parents realize that their teenage son or daughter is depressed, one of their first, biggest and most enduring fears is suicide. The vast majority of teens who kill themselves exhibit depressive symptoms, and many meet the criteria for a major depressive disorder. Other factors, like substance use and personality disorders, often coupled with depression, come into play as well.

Suicide rates are reported differently around the world, but even using a consistent method of reporting, it would be difficult to determine how many teens kill themselves. The required criteria for calling a death a suicide varies from province to province and from state to state. It's also possible that because of the social stigma attached to suicide, these deaths may be reported as having another cause (although there is no evidence that such misreporting occurs to any significant extent).

There are no routine statistics available on suicide attempts (also called parasuicide), adolescent or adult, although some studies have looked at the incidence of attempts in reasonably large groups of teens. One of these studies showed that around 2 percent of teens had tried to kill themselves, usually with methods that were unlikely to be lethal. Many studies have shown that girls are much more likely to attempt suicide, while boys are much more likely to actually kill themselves. Teens are less likely to die as a result of suicide attempts than adults. In a large Ontario study, about 12 percent of 12- to 16-year-olds reported some sort of suicidal thoughts (often referred to as suicidal ideation) or behavior, with girls being twice as likely as boys to report this.

In general, adolescents are not the age group most likely to commit suicide. Suicide rates go up with age, elderly white men being at highest risk in many countries. But because teens are unlikely to die from natural causes, suicide by teens stands out along with "accidental" injuries and homicide, as one of the chief ways teens tend to die. Adult suicides, although there are many more of them, are outnumbered by deaths from heart disease, cancer or other diseases.

Parents, relatives and friends all feel guilty when a teen commits suicide. Everyone thinks they should have known it was going to happen, should have reached out more, shouldn't have made critical comments. But a teen who is determined to kill himself will hide his intent and his plans, to make sure that no one will stop him; unplanned, impulsive suicidal acts are more common when teens have been drinking, and teen alcohol use is not usually something parents can control. Many suicides are triggered by a traumatic event (like a big fight with parents or a breakup with a boyfriend or girlfriend) but these things don't, in and of themselves, cause suicides.

This warning cannot be emphasized enough: *If your teen is depressed, lock up all medications that can kill in overdose.* This includes over-the-counter painkillers such as ASA and acetaminophen. Remove guns from the home. If you aren't prepared to do this, at least lock them up and lock up ammunition in a different place; hide the keys separately and not in the obvious places.

Warning Signs

James was 17. He had suffered from depression before and was now in the midst of his second bout. The first time it happened it hadn't seemed serious, so his parents wanted to watch for any signs that he was thinking about suicide. The trouble was, they didn't know what they should be watching for.

There are often (but not always) a number of warning signs that a teen is seriously considering suicide. By being on the lookout for them, you may be able to prevent a tragedy.

Hopelessness is a prominent aspect of depression in general, but if your son is expressing increasing feelings that nothing will ever change, that no one can help him, that he is a failure or that life is meaningless, you have grounds for concern and suspicion that he is at increased risk.

It may seem obvious, but the teen actually talking about suicide, even in a joking way, is another warning sign. Sometimes parents think that if their child talks about suicide, he won't actually try it, because if he really wanted to kill himself he would keep it secret. In fact, many kids who are thinking about suicide would like to be stopped. Take seriously any statements a teen makes about wanting to die, or any jokes he makes about who he would like at his funeral. If your son is talking about death or about a prominent figure (like a rock star) who has killed himself recently, it could be an indication that he himself is thinking about suicide.

Oddly enough, a sudden, distinct improvement in your son's mood may be another clue that he is planning a suicide.

A person who has made a definite plan and found the means to kill himself may feel relieved of a huge burden. He may thank the people around him for having been helpful, or he may apologize for having caused them problems. Of course, a worsening of the depression is also a reason for concern.

Teens who are planning to kill themselves may give away their possessions to friends or siblings. Unless your son makes a regular habit of divesting himself of the things he owns, this is a serious warning sign. Writing a will is a more sophisticated version of this.

A suicidal "gesture" like taking a few pills from the medicine cabinet may be a practice run. The trivial nature of the attempt does not indicate a lack of intent.

The association between substance (especially alcohol) abuse, depression and suicide is a strong one. You should be worried if your son is coming home drunk or smelling of alcohol.

Preventing a Suicide in a Depressed Teen

The first thing to be aware of is her mental state. Watch for warning signs and ask her how she is feeling. If you think she might be contemplating suicide, ask her about it. Watch for evasive answers ("Who would be dumb enough to do that?" or "You don't trust me") and persist until you get a real response.

If your child tells you she *is* thinking about killing herself, don't panic. She needs you to be able to reassure her and to help her cope with the situation. But don't act totally blasé either—you don't want her to get the idea that you don't care. Do not promise her that you won't tell anyone.

Let her know that you understand she must be in a great deal of emotional pain, but that you also know she will not always feel this way. Tell her that she does not have to feel guilty about this pain, that it isn't her fault. She does not need to feel ashamed of her pain or of her suicidal thoughts.

Tell her that she can be treated, that she will definitely feel better. Don't promise that the improvement will be immediate or even soon, but reassure her that you will be there to help her through the process. Make sure she knows that the way she is feeling is temporary, but that suicide is permanent.

Let your daughter know how much you love her and how devastating it would be to you and other family members if she killed herself. Tell her some specific ways she has enriched your life. Hold her hand, hug her, use your body language to show that you care.

Don't leave her alone. It only takes a moment to go into the bathroom and find a razor blade or a bunch of pills. You have probably already locked up or gotten rid of any lethal medications or firearms in the house. If not, get someone to do this while you stay with your daughter.

Ask your daughter to promise that she won't kill herself within a certain period of time.

Get her to make a promise she can keep. Don't ask her to promise never to kill herself. This is too big a thing for someone to commit to. She can say to herself, "I didn't know I would ever feel this bad when I told her that." Instead, get her to promise that she will talk with you, in person, before she attempts suicide. The "in person" part is important. You don't want her calling you from a pay phone or e-mailing you about this. This is a promise that many teens have made to parents or therapists and have kept.

Get help. If she says she has been thinking about killing herself but doesn't have a plan or doesn't think she would really do it, get her to a therapist, family doctor or pediatrician. If she has a more definite plan, exhibits some of the warning signs outlined above or cannot reassure you that she will not kill herself, take her to an emergency room.

Some Questions from Parents and Teachers about Suicide

My daughter, Ellie, is 16. A few months ago, when she was seriously depressed, she had thoughts of suicide. Recently she told me that she doesn't feel suicidal now, but she worries that the feeling might come back again. Right now, she wants to live, but when she gets depressed, it's hard for her to remember that things will get better. What can I do to help her?

Ellie is thinking ahead. She wants to make a plan to continue to live. She sounds as if she understands herself pretty well, which is a good first step. If she isn't seeing a therapist, find one for her. She could benefit from talking to a therapist about a plan to stay alive.

Write down the phone numbers of her therapist or doctor, a crisis phone line and a close friend who might help. Ask her to carry these numbers in her wallet, and to promise that she will use them if she needs them. Get her a prepaid phone card so that she will always have the means to call.

Ask her to tell you if she feels suicidal again. Make sure she knows that you want to help. Ask her to give you some advice about what might help.

Encourage her to track of how she is feeling. If she likes to write, suggest that she keep a journal. (Her journal is private, of course, but writing it might help her with talking about her feelings.) If she doesn't like to write, she might draw a picture every day that reflects her mood, or give herself a daily number rating on her calendar. If she sees a downward trend over several days in any of these, she can talk with you or her therapist.

Get rid of any firearms in the house. An important immediate risk factor is a gun in the home. Even when what seem to be reasonable safety precautions have been taken, a firearm in the home increases the risk of suicide for both male and female teens. One study that compared suicide rates in Seattle and Vancouver showed that the higher rates in Seattle mirrored the difference in gun ownership rates.

If there are lethal medications around, lock them up or dispose of them. Make sure your teen doesn't have a stash of such drugs from when she was suicidal before. If she does, flush them down the toilet now.

Ask her to write down what she would say to someone who was thinking about killing herself. What are good reasons for living? Remind her that suicidal feelings lift, and ask her to write a letter to herself, explaining that she will feel better. She can keep the letter and read it if she starts thinking about suicide.

Reassure her that her feelings are nothing to be ashamed of, and that there is no reason to be embarrassed about asking for help. Many people have felt suicidal and have gotten through it because of doctors and therapists who have been there to lend a helping hand.

Ask her to stay away from drugs and alcohol, especially when she is feeling down, because they can make her even sadder than she is. They can also trigger a suicide attempt by making her more impulsive.

Remind her to get in touch with nature. Suggest that she

go for walks in the woods, notice the wildlife and plants. This will help her to get some perspective, to calm down and to feel like a part of something larger than herself.

My son has been quite depressed, and I'm worried that he is going to try to kill himself. I have locked up all our medication, and I get up a few times during the night to check on him. I can't ask him if he is suicidal, because if he hasn't been thinking this way, I don't want him to get any ideas. What can I do?

It's good that you have locked up dangerous medications. If there are some that no one is using, you should just get rid of them. I'm sure that if you had any guns in the house you would have moved them out by now, too. As suicide can be a fairly impulsive act, it is good to remove very lethal possibilities from your son.

However, you cannot always prevent suicide by removing the means to accomplish it You can't get rid of every knife, rope or sheet that you own. You can't move from a twelfth-floor apartment into one farther down or away from a city that has a subway. People who are determined to kill themselves will usually find a way.

One thing you can do is to talk to your son. Chances are, if he is as depressed as he sounds, he has at least thought about killing himself. He has certainly heard about suicide, so you won't be giving him ideas that he wouldn't have thought of on his own.

It can be a real relief for a teen who is very depressed to be able to talk to a parent about suicidal feelings. He may have thought that he couldn't bring the subject up with you. He may feel better just talking about it.

Increasing Suicide Rates

I never heard about anyone killing themselves when I was in high school. Now my daughter tells me about friends talking about suicide and classmates being taken off in ambulances because they've tried to kill themselves in the bathroom. Judging from the fundraising mail I get, crisis and suicide hotlines are very busy also. Why are so many more kids doing this?

Since the early 1950s, suicide rates have doubled or tripled. Adolescent suicide is still a pretty uncommon event, and just as you never went to school with someone who killed himself, chances are your daughter also will not know anyone who commits suicide.

Depression rates are going up and we know that there is a definite link between suicide attempts and depression. In addition, depression seems to be occurring in younger and younger children. These girls and boys may not have developed the same strategies as older teens for dealing with uncomfortable feelings, and may be more likely to see suicide as a viable alternative.

With depression on the rise, thoughts of suicide are also more common. It is possible that teens are talking more about these thoughts than teens did in the past, when there was more of a stigma attached to suicide. Some well-known teen idols have killed themselves, and suicide is discussed in health classes and young adult fiction. In this new climate, adolescents may be more open about their feelings. Some teens may realize that talking about suicidal thoughts may get someone to pay attention to the pain they are feeling.

Your daughter may be telling you these things because she is confused or worried about suicide. She may want to talk about why someone would do this. She may feel responsible for preventing her friends from killing themselves. She may have had some suicidal thoughts herself and may be bringing up the topic to see how you react. If you can respond with comments that invite more discussion rather than shutting things down, you can help her figure things out.

Identifying the Suicidal Teen in a Large Group

I teach at a large high school. Last year one of our students killed himself. We were worried that we would end up with a suicide epidemic but, fortunately, this didn't happen. No one realized that this kid was in serious trouble at the time, and I feel bad that I never noticed that he was having problems. Are there ways we can pick out students who might try to kill themselves?

In the aftermath of this terrible event, many people, both students and teachers, will feel guilty and try to find ways to prevent it from happening to another student.

It is not easy to tell which teens in any given group are at risk of attempting or committing suicide, and no program will ever be completely successful. I am sure that since this happened, teachers at your school are making it clear to students that they can come to them for help, that the guidance department is helping teens find resources, and that students are providing (at least informal) peer support. Getting depressed teens to seek help through these channels themselves is likely to be more successful than attempting to identify at-risk students by outward signs. Also, I am sure your school has developed programs that focus on any particular issues that may have been involved in this student's suicide, such as substance abuse, bullying, homophobia or depression.

Many things put teens at risk of suicide. Certain aspects of their lives (discussed below) make it more likely that particular teens will kill themselves. Within these risk groups, it becomes much harder to predict who will actually attempt suicide, although the chance becomes greater with an increasing number of risk factors. Some teens who attempt or commit suicide have no risk factors, while many who have these factors do not ever attempt to kill themselves.

We can think of some risk factors as being more general, such as things from the past that have increased the teen's vulnerability to specific stressors or certain events that pose more immediate risks. I will refer to these risk factors as *foundation* risk factors.

In all age groups, psychiatric disorders (including substance abuse) are a strong foundation risk factor for suicide. Although depression predominates, personality disorders and substance abuse are also common risk factors for suicide; people who attempt suicide but survive are less likely to have one of these three problems than those who do not survive. Within these groups of psychiatric illnesses, those with the worst symptoms are the most likely to kill themselves.

Having more than one psychiatric diagnosis also increases the risk of suicide. Substance abuse is associated with more lethal methods, more frequent attempts and more serious suicidal intent. In addition to being a foundation risk, substance use also seems to be a more immediate risk, with half of teens who kill themselves being intoxicated at the time of death, almost always with alcohol and sometimes with other drugs added. Teachers may be able to identify students who are depressed or who are using substances.

A previous suicide attempt is another risk factor for a completed suicide, but this risk is not as strong for teens as it is for older people. Often, teens who have attempted suicide do not tell anyone about it, so it is hard to identify this group.

Another foundation risk seems to be decreased serotonin levels in the brain stem and prefrontal areas of the brain, but this factor has been found only on autopsy. It isn't clear whether low levels of neurotransmitters are directly linked to suicidal ideas and attempts, with higher levels protecting against depression and other psychiatric problems that are then related to suicide. The link may be more indirect, but although there is no evidence that a sudden drop in serotonin causes suicidal feelings, it is certainly a possibility. Obviously, low serotonin levels cannot be identified by school staff or parents.

The suicide of a family member increases the risk of the teen also killing himself. To a lesser extent, the risk also increases if a family member has a psychiatric problem. Poverty and other family problems, such as observed family violence and physical and sexual abuse of the teen, also increase the chance of suicide. Family violence is a foundation risk factor and can also be an immediate risk factor, with an episode of abuse precipitating suicide. Teachers may suspect a teen is suffering abuse, but are unlikely to know about other family violence.

A teen who was a friend of someone who committed suicide is at high risk for attempting or committing suicide.

Teens who live in rural areas are at higher risk of suicide. This is probably due to a number of factors, including higher levels of substance use, easier access to firearms and limited mental health resources. In addition, teens in rural areas who feel "different" in some way are more likely to feel isolated than those in larger centers.

Aboriginal youth are at high risk of suicide, both on and off reserves. Some of this may be due to rural factors, but poverty, isolation, marginalization and history all come into play.

When foundation factors exist, it is more likely that an immediate risk factor will precipitate a suicide attempt or provide the conditions needed for a suicide.

A major stressful event, such as the death of a parent or close friend, trouble with the police, incarceration or the end of a relationship may precipitate an actual suicide or a suicide attempt. Bullying can cause ongoing stress and also stimulate a suicide attempt. In some cases, the school will be aware of these events and in some instances a teen will confide in a teacher about life stresses.

Many suicide attempts and completed suicides are precipitated by a fight with a romantic partner, close friend or parent.

Experiences of sexual or physical assault, either within or outside the family, are also immediate risk factors.

Teachers should always take any talk about suicide seriously. If a teen has attempted suicide by a method that is clearly non-lethal, there is a tendency to minimize the importance of any further mention of suicide. Teens do not always know what will kill them and may make another attempt when the first one fails. In my opinion, talk of suicide is always a request for help.

Can You Always Tell If Someone Is Suicidal?

There was an article in the paper recently about a man who killed himself. It was discovered that he had been planning his suicide for several months, writing down how he would do it, stockpiling medications, even rehearsing the event.

I know that parents can't know what their child is thinking, but surely once someone moves into active planning like this, it must be pretty obvious what is going on.

Not everyone who kills himself progresses through the careful planning that this man did. We don't entirely understand the process that occurs in a teen that leads to suicide. Teens who have attempted suicide have been interviewed extensively, but they are not always aware of their feelings and thought processes before the attempt, and they may be very different from teens who actually kill themselves.

Some theorists have looked at how suicidal thoughts progress toward suicidal behavior. Many teens have some suicidal musings at some time. These may be as mild as wondering how people would react if they were dead, or who would come to their funeral. Others might contemplate suicide out of anger, seeing it as a way to get revenge on their parents. However, suicide in a teen is not always the result of a continuum that moves from idea to plan to action, although it may be so for many adults. Impulsivity probably plays a role in many teen suicides and the ideation, planning and attempt may take place almost simultaneously. In a case like this, parents would have no warning.

Suicidal thoughts and behaviors can be seen as a pyramidal structure. At the base, large numbers of teens think about killing themselves at some point. Moving up the pyramid, fewer teens seriously consider suicide and even fewer develop a plan. A much smaller number attempt to kill themselves with a method that is unlikely to result in death, still fewer attempt suicide with a potentially lethal method. For every teen who kills himself, there are thousands of teens at the bottom of the pyramid, with several hundred who seriously contemplate suicide and one hundred who try it. It can be reassuring to consider how few teens there are at the top of the structure, the ones who actually do kill themselves. However, each loss of a young person is significant and for every teen who dies, many more have been miserable or angry enough to seriously contemplate suicide.

Why Do Teens Kill Themselves?

A girl in our town committed suicide recently. She did well in school and came from a family with plenty of money. I just don't get why a kid who has her whole life ahead of her would kill herself.

I don't think any of us can really understand why someone commits suicide. Many teens with multiple risk factors don't ever attempt or commit suicide. What drives any teen to the brink is hard to pinpoint. However, when depression is a factor, things like good grades and money can seem meaningless to the teenager.

I don't think any teen really wants to be dead. Many get to the point where life seems too painful to continue, and death, being "not-life," seems like the only alternative. Even though they know that death is permanent, they may see it more as a rest or a break when everything has become too much. Ironically, a suicide plan can sometimes keep a teen going a bit longer. He can see that he will get the rest, and it makes life more bearable in the shorter term.

Hopelessness, common in depression, can be a major precipitant. If a teen truly feels there is no chance that the future will be any different, he will see no reason to live. Instilling hope is often an essential part of treating depressed teens. Without hope, any solutions or alternatives that are suggested will be rejected.

Teens who are considering suicide often describe feeling overwhelmed by life events and their situation in general. Sometimes breaking down their problems into pieces and helping them find a solution to even one piece can help.

A sudden impulse can often lead a teen to a suicidal act. Impulsive suicide is often associated with alcohol or drug use, but can also occur without it. The teen suddenly sees suicide as the answer. He may feel an urge to drive his car into a tree or to jump off a building without even thinking about death or suicide.

Unexpected Suicide

Our neighbor's son shot and killed himself last year. His parents are still trying to figure it out. He did not seem to be depressed and had never talked about suicide. Was he just hiding his problems well?

Although it may very well be that this young man was depressed and hiding it, up to 10 percent of teens who kill themselves have no history of any psychiatric problem and show no signs of depression in the weeks before their death.

Teens without depression who kill themselves are more likely than the average teen to have been in trouble with the law or at school. These problems are not usually a precipitating event, although it could be that some of these teens are worried about getting into trouble again. I think these legal and school problems are more likely a reflection of impulsivity. Impulsive teens are more likely to have been arrested, and a suicidal thought may be impulsively acted upon. Alcohol use may be linked, both as a reason for previous difficulties and also with loosening inhibitions at the time of the suicide.

Some studies suggest that teens who are gay or who are worrying about sexual orientation issues are more likely to try to kill themselves. These attempts usually happen before the teen has told any family members or close friends, and so interviews with families afterwards would not reveal this as a cause of suicide.

The presence of any gun in the house, and especially a loaded one, seems to be strongly related to suicide in non-depressed teens. Again, a major stressful event (a relationship breaking up, bullying at school) could lead to suicidal thoughts, and an impulsive teen who has access to a lethal means of suicide might use a weapon without thinking things through.

There is also some evidence that non-depressed teens who commit suicide are more likely to have a family member with a psychiatric disorder. It isn't clear whether the suicide is related to the stress of living with someone who is depressed or who has other serious problems or whether there is a biological predisposition to suicidal thoughts and actions in this group.

Can Treatment Lead to Suicide?

I have read that people are more likely to commit suicide when they are getting treatment. Is this true? If so, wouldn't my son be better off just waiting for his depression to pass, rather than going to a therapist or taking drugs?

Thoughts about death, contemplation of suicide and actually planning a suicide attempt are all associated with depression and, of course, with suicide itself. Neither psychotherapy nor medication have instant results, and we certainly wouldn't expect a lower suicide rate early in treatment. In fact, as you have read, the risk of suicide does go up early in treatment with psychotherapy and medication, at least in adults. A profoundly depressed teen who doesn't understand that treatment will take time to work might feel that she cannot be helped when she does not feel any better after two or three weeks. In addition, therapy may involve discussing painful subjects, and someone may actually feel worse after leaving a therapy session.

Some antidepressants are toxic if an overdose is taken. As medication also does not provide instant relief, a teen who feels he is not getting better on medication might feel hopeless and have the means at hand to kill himself. Older antidepressants (tricyclics) can be used to commit suicide. They are not often prescribed for teens because of this danger, but if they are used, they should be dispensed in small amounts so that they cannot be used for an overdose. Newer antidepressants have much lower toxicity, but large amounts still should not be given out, especially early in treatment.

There is concern that some medications may actually lead to suicidal thoughts. Benzodiazepines (not usually used in depression) may be associated with an increased risk of suicide. There has also been speculation and a bit of research about amitriptyline (a tricyclic antidepressant) increasing suicide risk. There seems to be some variability in suicide risk early in treatment with SSRIs, with some of them decreasing suicide risk and others leaving it at the same levels as in untreated patients.

Given all this, why get treatment for your son? This possible increased risk of suicide occurs early in treatment, but over time treatment does help, and a teen who is not depressed is much less likely to kill himself than one who is. Also, a teen who is depressed feels miserable. His academic, social and family life are all affected. A teen with depression has a reasonably good chance of recovering without intervention, but it can take a long time and he suffers in the meantime. Not all teens can recover on their own, so you might end up having to help him get treatment anyway after watching him be depressed for five or six months.

Researchers are also speculating that teens who are treated early in their first bout of depression are less likely to go on to subsequent depressions. If this is true, this would be another reason for your son to get treatment.

Homosexuality and Suicide

I organize recreational activities at a community center. I have heard that gay teens are at high risk of suicide, although the ones I've met have been pretty well adjusted. So, is this a myth, or am I fooling myself?

The vast majority of gay teens do not commit suicide, and may come to terms with their minority sexual orientation without major angst. However, a number of studies have shown that gay teens are more likely to think about, plan and attempt suicide than heterosexual teens. There seem to be significant differences between suicide attemptors and people who actually kill themselves, so we cannot draw the conclusion that gay and lesbian teens are more likely to kill themselves. However, it is known that gay teens who attempt suicide tend to use highly lethal methods in their attempts. Suicide attempts in gay people are at their peak during the adolescent years. This vulnerability is probably a result of their struggles with issues of sexuality, isolation and identity.

One way that researchers determine why someone committed suicide is to do a "psychological autopsy." Family members and friends are interviewed, and any diary or suicide note is examined. If no one in the family was aware that the teen was gay, and he didn't write about it, this factor would not show up in any of these studies. In addition, the possibility would not be raised unless the investigator was specifically looking for it, and until recently most researchers weren't doing so. Thus, it's unlikely that a psychological autopsy would identify an isolated teen as gay if she had no connections with the gay community and hadn't come out to friends or family. We know that most gay teens who attempt suicide do so without having disclosed their sexual orientation to family or friends, but for those who succeed in killing themselves the statistics are unreliable for all the reasons stated above.

If there is an increased risk of suicide in these teens, it seems probable that those at highest risk are the adolescents who feel they cannot tell anyone that they think they may be gay. They may feel as though a terrible thing has happened to them and that there is no hope for a normal life.

A particularly vulnerable group comprise those who appear or behave differently from same-sex peers (regardless of their actual sexual orientation). These adolescents get teased, bullied and physically harassed because other teens think they are gay.

An additional risk is that when many young gay people are looking for a community, the only place they can find is a gay bar, even if they are living in a big city. Bars and alcohol consumption go hand in hand, and drinking is often associated with adolescent suicides.

We do know that many young gays and lesbians feel isolated, ashamed and very unhappy. If no one knows they are gay, they hear homophobic comments aimed at others by both teachers and their peers. If they are out, they suffer directly from those comments and often from threats to their physical safety. Some parents are very unsupportive, and if their teen tells them that she is gay they may even kick her out of the house. Whether these teens are at high risk of killing themselves or not, they need information, support and opportunities to meet other young gay people.

Personality Disorders and Suicide

> *My 16-year-old daughter's therapist says he's pretty*
> *sure she has borderline personality disorder. Although*
> *he didn't say things were hopeless, he painted a bleak*
> *picture, including a high risk that she will kill herself*
> *at some point. We are very shaken by this. Is this true*
> *and what can we do to prevent it?*

Although borderline personality disorder is a serious diagnosis, it is important to remember that the earlier a psychiatric problem is treated, the better the chances of recovery. Also, it is difficult to diagnose personality disorders in teens, as adolescents are still developing psychologically.

Several personality disorders are associated with an increased risk of suicide, including antisocial personality disorder and borderline personality disorder, but a diagnosis of borderline personality disorder does not mean that your daughter will kill herself.

This condition is very hard to treat, for a number of reasons. A few programs have pioneered intensive treatment of personality disorders, but not very many therapists have developed expertise in this area. Because a personality disorder is deep-rooted and involves long-term treatment, people who are interested in providing briefer types of therapy do not usually have much success with these teens. Teens with this problem tend to get very attached to people who are helping them and often imagine that their relationship with them is much more intimate than it really is. They then end up feeling betrayed when they find out that their therapist is not really their "friend," and move on to another therapist, who has to start all over again.

Although the research in this area is not entirely clear, it seems that as many as 30 to 40 percent of people who commit suicide have a personality disorder, often coexisting with depression or substance abuse. The risk of suicide in people with borderline personality disorder seems to be higher after adolescence, perhaps when life seems to take on a pattern of rejection and other disappointments. However, the majority of people with personality disorders do not kill themselves.

Suicide attempts should be taken seriously. A young person with a personality disorder may be desperate for help that she feels she cannot get in any way except by a suicide attempt. Even if there is no real suicidal intent, death can still result from an attempt.

The best thing you can do for your daughter is to try to find a program that has been successful in treating young people with personality disorders. If you can't find one, talk with her therapist and see how comfortable he is in continuing to care for her. It may be especially important to focus on three things: social skills, interpersonal problem solving and treatment of any coexisting depression. Knowing that your daughter will probably want to switch therapists frequently, figure out in advance (perhaps with the help of her therapist) what to do when she expresses this need. Report signs of depression or substance abuse to the therapist so that these can be treated appropriately.

Race and Suicide

I've never heard of a black teen committing suicide, but my 14-year-old niece is depressed and I have been very worried about her killing herself. Do black kids kill themselves, or can I stop worrying about suicide?

There is no group of adolescents who are totally protected from suicide, no matter what their ethnic background. Your niece is less likely to kill herself than a nephew, but this certainly doesn't mean that it can't happen. Likewise, suicide rates for black teens in the United States have always been lower than for white teens. Unfortunately, it seems that the rate of suicide among young black males is on the upswing (at least, it was until the mid-1990s, when studies were done). These rates vary between geographic regions.

A number of people have come up with reasons why young black people seem to be less likely to kill themselves, including a greater degree of religious observance and belief, the possibility that black suicides are underreported and a (fortunate) lack of black "suicide role models." None of these theories have been proven; in fact, it would be hard to prove or disprove any of them.

Studies that have looked at suicidal ideation show that teens from all ethnic groups think about suicide. I am aware of only one study that looked at risk factors associated with completed suicides in African-Americans. This study compared adults who had killed themselves with others, similar in gender, age, race and educational level, who had died of natural causes. A number of risk factors were found for the white subjects—heavy drinking, lower level of education, use of mental health services or blue-collar jobs. However, only one risk factor was identified for the black subjects—past use of mental health services. This was seen as an indicator of a mental health problem, such as depression.

No matter what the statistics, your niece is a unique individual, and no research study is going to tell you whether she will try to kill herself. If she is already getting help, your job is to be there to support and love her. If she is not getting therapy or medication, you can assist her in finding services and encourage her to get treatment. It seems that you are close. You could address the issue of suicide. Let her know that you have been worried. You may want to ask her to promise you that she won't try to kill herself without talking to you first. Tell her how important she is to you.

Are Ideas about Suicide Catching?

> *Our 13-year-old daughter has a close friend who is depressed and talks about death quite a bit. I have heard that there are often outbreaks of suicide, and I am wondering if I should forbid Jodie to spend time with this girl.*

"Clusters" of suicides have been reported for many years. These are suicides that happen close together in time, often with the same method and usually in geographical proximity. Clusters may also occur in non-geographical groupings, such as among fans of a rock star who committed suicide. Clusters of teen suicides seem to have increased in the past decade.

A young person who is experiencing psychological pain, and who can think of no way out, may see the suicide of another person as a model of how to escape her torment, especially if she identifies with the person in some way. She may have been contemplating suicide, but not have known how to do it, and the "successful" suicide may then be seen as instructive. A suicidal teen may feel challenged by hearing of a suicide at her school or in the community—"If he can do it, then so can I."

The majority of teens who kill themselves have an underlying psychiatric problem, usually depression or substance abuse. If your daughter does not have one of these conditions and is not particularly impulsive, she is at low risk of killing herself.

Forbidding Jodie to see her friend is not likely to be helpful. Teens tend to resist such injunctions and feel that they should be able to choose their own friends.

Is your daughter this girl's only source of support through her experience of depression and suicidal feelings? This is not a burden Jodie should be carrying. Her friend needs adult, professional help now. Perhaps you could help her by talking to her or her parents about what is going on, finding out about affordable resources in your community or encouraging her to call a crisis line.

What Can I Do to Help the Parent after a Suicide?

The worst happened to my best friend. Her son killed himself a month ago. I feel as if there is nothing I can do. At first I was able to help with the funeral arrangements and cook for her family. Now, when I see her, I have nothing to offer. I try not to mention her son because I am sure it hurts her to think about him. We used to go out for a walk every Sunday night, but she seems so down that I'm sure she wouldn't want to.

It is hard to know what to say or do for anyone who has lost a child and even harder when the death is by suicide. But there is quite a bit you can do for your friend.

You need to understand that your friend is grieving intensely. The sudden, unexpected loss of her son feels worse to her than waking up missing her arms or legs. She is thinking about him all the time, so you don't have to worry that bringing up his name or talking about your memories of him will make things worse. She might think that you are avoiding talking about him because you blame her for his suicide. People who are grieving often welcome an opportunity to talk about the person who has died.

She doesn't have to sit around crying all the time. She may welcome an opportunity to start your walks again, for both the exercise and the company. It's okay to bring up the topics you usually discuss, including your own children.

Is there a reason that you can no longer offer meals to the family? Many people eat poorly after a family member has died, but will eat if someone provides food. It may also be helpful for you to be able to provide something as tangible as sustenance for the family.

Even though your friend doesn't have to cry, it's all right if she wants to. Crying is a powerful way to express and deal with emotions. As her best friend, you probably know what to do when she cries, whether she would like you to put an arm around her, hand her a tissue or just let her deal with it. If you don't know what to do, you can ask.

If your friend wants to talk about why her son died, that's fine, but let her choose to talk about it when she wants to. It is probably not helpful to wonder out loud why he would have killed himself. If she blames herself for his death, you can assure her that it isn't her fault.

Everyone grieves differently, depending on their previous experiences of death, their personality and usual coping style, their relationship with the person who died and many other factors. Because there is no right or wrong way to grieve, part of your job as a friend is to accept her way of dealing with her son's death.

If there are other children in the family, they may be feeling shut out by their parents' grief. If you are close to any of them, you could invite them out for a walk or over for a meal.

People who are grieving experience a number of common symptoms: loss of appetite, fatigue, frequent crying and feelings of sadness and anger. People who have lost a child to suicide may also feel ashamed, rejected by their child and responsible for the death. By being aware of this, you may be able to help your friend realize that she isn't responsible for the suicide and that she does not need to feel ashamed. If you do blame your friend for not realizing that her son was suicidal, for having the means available in her house or for any other reason, work out these feelings with your spouse, a counselor or someone else you trust. Expressing these things to your grieving friend will not help either her or your relationship.

12. Question Period

During my years of treating adolescents and advising their parents I've been asked questions about many aspects of teen depression. Here are some I have heard, some from teens, some from parents, about living with depression.

Questions from Teens

My mother knows that I have been depressed lately and she has been pretty supportive, but there is one thing that drives me nuts. I find it really helpful to keep a journal and write about how I am feeling. She thinks that this is "morose" and that I am just "wallowing in my misery." She came to my room last night to talk to me, and I asked her if she could just wait a minute while I finished writing. She got pissed off and told me that human relations are more important than a diary. How can I explain to her how much writing helps me?

I think there is more than one thing going on here. To start with, I think your mother felt hurt that you would want to write in your journal instead of talking to her. She might have felt inadequate, that it was a reflection on her parenting skills that you prefer to "talk" to your diary.

Second, I think she forgets what it is like to be a teen with a diary. The journal is almost like another person, one who is totally safe to talk to. This sense of the diary as a person is what makes Anne Frank's diary come to life, why we feel that she is speaking to us when we read it.

But also your mother doesn't seem to understand how helpful writing can be. It is a process with great healing powers, and if she has never used writing in this way, she might not be able to guess how you feel about it. Try to explain to her that the diary doesn't replace her or your friends, but that you do find writing in it helpful and that you feel better afterwards.

At the same time, you might also want to think about how to use your writing to its full potential. Here are some ideas.

Set aside some time each day to write. Make sure that you don't skip writing because you are feeling okay and don't "need to." When you are feeling really down and are sure that things have always been terrible and will never improve, you can read some of your entries from when things were better.

When you are done writing, read over what you have written. See if the statements you have made about yourself are rational extensions of the event that led to them. If you spilled grape juice on your white shirt and wrote, "I am so stupid," you are drawing an unjustified conclusion. Use a different colored pen to write in a new conclusion, like, "That was a really clumsy thing to do."

Look to see if you have used the words "always" or "never" or others that mean the same things, and again check to see if they apply. If there are any exceptions to them, change the word to something less harsh.

If your rereading suggests an action you could take to help you feel better, write that down too.

Give each day a rating after you have written. On a scale of one to ten, if one was that you were about to actually kill yourself and ten is the best day you have ever had, where on that scale does today fit? It can be useful to go back and look at this rating over the course of a week or a month.

Remember that you are not Anne Frank and that your diary will not be published. Don't worry about grammar, spelling or neatness and don't imagine any audience except, perhaps, your adult self.

Keep your journal somewhere safe. If you leave it on the coffee table in the living room, your mother might very well think that this is a hint that you would like her to read it. You certainly don't want your younger brother to read it or to show it to his friends.

When I'm really down, I just can't handle being around a lot of people. My mother made me go to a bar mitzvah last week, and it was terrible. But she says I'm turning agoraphobic and need to get out. What do you think?

This is a real dilemma. It is difficult to get out and to be around large groups of people when you are depressed. You can end up feeling more alone and isolated than you would if you were by yourself. On the other hand, it isn't a good idea to spend all your time holed up.

It is important that you get treatment for your depression. Although many teens with major depression get better on their own over six to twelve months, this is too long to suffer.

Once you are getting treatment, after the first few weeks you should probably push yourself to get out with a small number of friends. Avoid large gatherings (one solution for the bar mitzvah might have been to go to the service but skip the party) and people you don't know well. Start off with a couple of friends in a casual setting (like your living room or theirs) who know you haven't been feeling well. Don't choose the people who tell you to "just cheer up" as the first people to see. Don't drink or smoke dope while socializing—these things may make you feel more depressed. Let your friends know in advance that you might not be up for a late night.

Ever since I told my mother that I was thinking about killing myself, she doesn't seem to be able to leave me alone. I appreciated her help at the time, maybe she even saved my life. But now she comes and checks on me during the night, asks me several times a day how I am feeling and wants me to come home right after school or check in frequently if I am out with friends. She even offered to buy me a cellular phone so she could stay in touch with me! How can I get her to calm down?

It is obvious that your mother is very worried about you. That's part of her job as a parent. She may also have started off as an anxious person and could be lying awake at night with her fears about your safety gnawing away at her.

If you are like most people, you have probably responded to her solicitousness with annoyance, something that might be satisfying at the time but is unlikely to change her behavior. Try to explain calmly to her that you appreciated her help when you were depressed and that you are glad you could talk to her. Let her know that because you are feeling so much better now, you are trying to get on with your life and trying not to dwell on how you were feeling before. Tell her that you will let her know if you start to feel suicidal again. Assure her that you do not need to be checked on during the night and that you need to have uninterrupted sleep.

If she is an anxious person in general, you might try weaning her off her worrying. Offer to check in with her once a day for two weeks at a specific time to tell her briefly how you are doing. After two weeks make it every two days, then every three days. After that, set up a time once a week when the two of you can go out for coffee or for a walk. You have no obligation to tell her everything about your life or your feelings, but she will feel better if she feels she has regular contact with you, and you will probably enjoy it too.

As I said, parents are supposed to worry and, if you cut yourself off from her in exasperation, she will worry even more.

My doctor gave me drugs so that I wouldn't be so depressed. I've been on them for one week and feel just as down, but I also feel queasy every evening. Why should I take something that makes me feel worse?

Side effects can be a real drag, but I hope your doctor told you that you might experience nausea and that it is temporary. You should not stop taking your medication without talking to your doctor first. Remember, many people take a month to show a response to antidepressants.

Nausea and other side effects may be due to the drug or could be coincidental. Serious side effects should be reported to your doctor right away. But there may be side effects that the doctor warned you about and said would go away after a week or two that do not need to be reported immediately. There may still be tricks to help improve how you are feeling, instead of just waiting for these effects to disappear.

Nausea is one of the most commonly reported side effects of SSRIs. It often comes on within an hour of taking the medication and goes away an hour or two later. Some SSRIs are taken with supper, because their absorption is improved by food. If you feel nauseated in the evening, you could take your medication closer to bedtime with a snack and will hopefully be asleep by the time the nausea hits. Antinausea pills should not be taken unless they are approved by the prescribing doctor. Two natural remedies for nausea are ginger tea (grate some fresh ginger into a teapot, pour boiling water over it and let it steep for at least five minutes) and sniffing alcohol (rubbing or drinking—just put some on a cotton ball and smell it).

A side effect such as dry mouth can be very distressing, and it can also make you appear weird to others if you run your tongue along your gums, swallow frequently or have difficulty talking. Drinking lots of water can help, and you can carry a water bottle to classes or in your knapsack when you go out. Brushing your teeth after every meal and at bedtime helps too. If you can't brush after lunch because there is nowhere private (I know everyone would think you are a nerd if they saw you brushing your teeth), try to at least rinse out your mouth and maybe eat an apple. Chewing sugarless gum can also help. Avoid sugared gum and hard candies that can cause cavities.

Constipation is a common problem in adolescents anyway and can be a side effect of antidepressants. Drinking lots of water and increasing fiber in your diet by eating a high-bran cereal in the morning and snacking on popcorn, fruits or vegetables will help.

Dizziness, as a side effect, can often be prevented by changing positions slowly. It helps if you sit up in the morning for a couple of minutes before standing, or wiggle your feet before going from sitting to standing.

Blurred vision is an uncommon side effect that is very worrisome to people who experience it, some of whom wonder if they are going blind. The cause of this blurring is not known. It may be that the tiny muscles that control the ability to focus are sluggish with these drugs. There are no reports of anyone losing their sight or having any permanent problems as a result of taking antidepressants. If your vision is blurred for more than two weeks and does not seem to be improving, you should let your doctor know. A change of medication may be in order.

Drowsiness with antidepressants is usually a passing thing. If it occurs, you may need to sleep more for a week or so. Avoid tech and sewing or cooking classes (you don't want to hurt yourself) and get your parents to drive you places until the drowsy spells pass. If you are taking your medication in the morning, try switching to suppertime.

Sleep problems can occur with antidepressants. If they do not resolve within a week or two, your doctor should consider changing your medication. Insomnia can sometimes be helped by a hot bath about an hour before bedtime, early evening exercise or a glass of hot milk at bedtime. If you think the medication is making it hard for you to fall asleep, you should take it in the morning rather than in the evening.

Agitation is scary for both teens and parents alike. If you are feeling antsy or jittery or can't seem to stay still when you're on medication, you should let your doctor know, especially if this feeling lasts more than a day. It is not serious in the traditional sense (it won't kill you or cause permanent disability), but it is so distressing that I think it should be dealt with right away.

I was depressed, and in addition to a prescription, my family doctor suggested family therapy. He said that if my family could come it could help me feel better. My

parents weren't all that keen on the idea, but they said
they would go if the doctor thought it was important.
In the sessions, the therapist seemed to be dwelling
on my dad's mood quite a bit. My father has always
been a kind of gloomy guy, and he was having a lot of
trouble with his boss at the time, but my mom and
dad both thought we should be concentrating on **my**
problems, not his. I wonder, is he depressed and is his
depression causing mine?

It may be that when you were speaking with your family
doctor you communicated some worries about your father, and
this may have given him the idea to suggest family therapy. Or
he may have already had concerns about your dad's state of
mind and saw this as a way to treat the whole family together.

It is likely that your family doctor really did think that
family therapy would be helpful to you. In family therapy, the
idea is to look at the family as a system, or as an organism.
Every person's function affects all the other family members.
Family therapists sometimes talk about the "identified
patient," which would be you in this case, but really see the
whole family as the patient. If the therapist thinks your father
is depressed, it would be important to deal with it in the therapy, even if he doesn't think it is causing your depression.

On a few occasions, I have seen a young person who is
feeling depressed, only to find that the real depression exists
in another family member. In some cases it is simply that living with someone who is depressed can be a profoundly
depressing experience. In others, I have wondered if the teen
has unconsciously taken on depressive symptoms as a way to
get help or attention for the person who is depressed. With
one of these teens, the parents felt that it was all right for a
child to get psychological help, but not for adults to go for

therapy, because they should be able to "pull themselves out of it" without going outside the family.

Whatever is going on with you and your family, it sounds as if your father does not want to accept that he could have a psychological problem. It is likely that he will stop going for family therapy unless the therapist switches the focus to your problems, at least for a while.

Even if your father's problems are affecting you, a therapist should be able to help you deal with your depression and the effect that your father's depression is having on you.

Questions from Parents

Sometimes my daughter says that I make her depressed because I nag her so much. I hate to think that her depression could all be my fault. How do I deal with this?

No one can *make* someone else depressed. You can tell her you understand that when she is feeling bad she might want to find something or someone to blame it all on, but those accusations are not going to help her feel better.

Many of us nag our kids when we are worried about them. If you are nagging her a lot, try to imagine how this might affect someone who is feeling hopeless. It might feed into her feelings of inadequacy, and she might feel guilty about not being the kind of daughter you deserve. She might start to be reluctant to tell you how she is feeling if she thinks you will just "get on her case" about it.

Some depressed people get into thinking in absolutes, like "I always mess up," or "I'll never feel any better." It will be helpful if you avoid this kind of terminology around your daughter, both when talking about her ("You never clean up your room when I ask you") or about yourself ("I'll never get promoted"). Try to model a positive approach. It won't cure her depression, but it might make her life a little easier, and you might end up with more positive feelings about her and about yourself.

My daughter seems so down on herself. If she does something well, she says it was easy—anyone could have done it. She blows things out of proportion, so that if she has a small failure, she feels like a total failure. She's always saying, "I should have done it differently." She wasn't like this before she got depressed. I tell her not to be so negative, but it doesn't seem to help. How can I convince her to be less hard on herself?

These kinds of thoughts often accompany a depression and can make recovery difficult. People who are thinking in these ways often don't even notice when they are feeling a bit better, but when they are having a tougher time, they see it as proof that they will never get better.

If your daughter is seeing a therapist, he might be addressing some of these thinking patterns, especially if he does cognitive therapy.

I don't think that parents should try to be therapists to their kids, but I do think that you can help your daughter find some strategies that might help.

Suggest a reality check. She says that the test was easy, and that's why she got an A. Did everyone in the class get an A? Did she hear people complaining about some of the questions or saying the test was too hard? Ask to see the test if she got it back and point out ways in which it might have been more difficult than she thought. Suggest that it seemed easy because of her ability to think through the answers or think laterally or whatever else might have helped.

Ask her what she would say to a friend who was saying the same thing about herself. When Joanne's boyfriend split up with her, did your daughter think it was because she was a loser who was totally unlovable? Or did she think that Mike was a jerk or that their differing interests made it difficult for them to sustain a relationship? (Make sure you pick an example where you know your daughter didn't think her friend was a failure.)

Ask her if anything good came out of the situation in which she failed. If she thinks she's stupid because the teacher made a negative comment on her paper, see if she learned anything from it or if she can come up with a rebuttal. Partial success, such as when she was hoping for an A but got a B, can be pointed out.

Suggest that she survey her friends. She says that John didn't ask her out because she is so boring. If you are pretty sure this isn't the case and that her friends really are friends, she can ask them if this seems to be a likely reason that he didn't ask her out.

Notice that none of these things relies solely on your opinion. Our kids (depressed or not) tend to disbelieve us when we say, "You are a beautiful young woman, and someday all of those kids will realize it," or "I'm sure that many of the people in your class really like you."

I drive my 14-year-old son to see his therapist every week. She says hello to me, but I never get a chance to find out what my son has said to her. I worry that he is going to tell her that he is going to kill himself and that I won't even know about it. Is everything between my son and his therapist confidential?

I understand how difficult it is to know that your son is talking to someone for an hour every week and that you have no idea what is going on. In addition to worrying that you might not hear about thoughts of suicide, you might also wonder what he is saying about you and what kind of opinion the therapist has formed about you and your family. Some parents feel jealous that their child, who may have been communicating only in grunts with them, seems to find enough to say for an hour of therapy every week. Others think that since they are paying for the therapy, they deserve regular updates.

The ground rules should have been established at the beginning. The relationship between a therapist and patient/client is confidential. This means that, other than in a few circumstances, the therapist will not, indeed cannot, tell you what your son has talked about, unless he gives his permission.

Some therapists will meet with parents every month or so, but they will usually use these sessions to get information from the parents about how things are going at home. If the child has given permission, the therapist might share some information. Parents can expect some generalities about how things are going, but nothing specific.

What are the exceptions to confidentiality? If your teen has been physically or sexually abused, in most places there is a legal requirement that it be reported to child welfare authorities. There is usually an age associated with this requirement, but it varies from one jurisdiction to the next. Most therapists also will talk to the police if a client tells them that they plan to kill someone, although this is not always legally required. If a therapist has serious concerns about your son attempting suicide, she is also required to intervene. This intervention will involve telling you what is going on, although you might get a call from her asking you to meet her at an emergency department or a call from a crisis worker at your local hospital.

It is likely that you drive your son to the therapist for a practical reason—so that he only misses a bit of school or because there is no reliable public transportation he can use. If this isn't the case, you should stop torturing yourself by sitting in the waiting room and hoping for a crumb of information. Let him get to the therapist himself and use the time for something that will help make you feel better.

> *Our daughter just joined a swim team. She was quite depressed a couple of months ago, and our family doctor started her on an antidepressant. She also goes to him for counseling. She is feeling much better (she certainly wasn't swimming two months ago) and is taking an interest in life again.*
>
> *Her new coach sent home a form with a letter that said that he needed to know about any medications the swimmers are on, as drugs could affect their performance or be picked up on drug testing. She doesn't want him to know that she is on a "psycho medicine." I can see her point. If she tells, he knows she's been depressed and might treat her differently.*
>
> *Our family doctor says there is no problem with swimming and the medication she is on. The local swimming organization says that it isn't a banned substance. What should we do?*

I'm sure the coach thinks this is a simple request. He just wants to know what medications the kids are taking. It may not have occurred to him that disclosure of drugs will often disclose a diagnosis. There are many medical and psychological problems that a teen may want to keep private. Sometimes this isn't possible. Some medications and conditions should be disclosed to a coach because they could interfere with the sport, or a teen could have a sudden, severe problem while participating in the sport.

It gets to be hard when you and your daughter would have to lie to protect her privacy. It also means that, from the beginning, your daughter has a secret from the coach—not the best way to establish a trusting relationship.

You could just tell your daughter that you have to tell the truth. But she has already made it quite clear that she does not want her coach to have this information.

In this situation I would put the generic name of the drug, not the more recognizable trade name, on the form. I would then pick one of your daughter's most prominent symptoms of her depression and put it in brackets after the name, such as "for sleep problems," or "for chronic fatigue problems," and maybe write a note saying that you have checked and it is an allowed substance. Hopefully the coach will not check into this any further.

> *We have to go through our HMO for all of our medical care. They say that for depression, they cover regular visits to a family doctor for antidepressant medication and that's it. Our family doctor seems genuinely concerned about our son, but isn't given enough time to do counseling or therapy. Private psychotherapists in our area charge a minimum of $75 an hour, which we can't afford. Are there any less expensive ways to get counseling or therapy?*

Financial coverage for mental health services is a problem for people in many places. Private insurers and health maintenance organizations (in the United States) have rules that are aimed at keeping costs down and are not always in the best interests of patients. In countries with better systems of medical care, mental health resources that are paid for may be limited to certain professions such as psychiatrists and psychologists.

Access problems can also arise in smaller or more remote communities where there are fewer mental health professionals.

There are some lower-cost solutions, but don't accept a service if it seems to be a bad fit for your teen or if you have hesitations about the therapist.

Group therapy may be one solution. Because a number of people are being helped at the same time, the cost may be less. There are usually two group leaders, so in a group with eight teens, the cost might be as low as $20 a session at a community agency. Group therapy can be quite helpful, as teens give each other feedback and support one another.

If you are a member of a church, synagogue, temple or other religious organization, they may offer pastoral counseling, either free or at a low cost. Make sure that the person who is offering this service is appropriately trained.

Some school systems have psychologists or counselors who are available to students. They may not be able to offer regular therapy, but they might be able to meet regularly with your teen, perhaps to review journal entries or discuss current issues.

Local service organizations may offer youth counseling. Try calling the YM/YWCA, Planned Parenthood or another such group. Even if they don't do counseling themselves, they may be aware of resources in your community.

If you live near a university, community college or psychotherapy training institute, they may offer lower rates for therapy with students. These people will have already had classroom teaching about therapy. They are closely supervised and will discuss your teen and the therapy with an experienced teacher.

Of course, if you are feeling really political, you could try to fight your HMO on this issue. They should be offering more than medication in treating troubled teens and adults.

My son seems to be feeling a bit better and is trying to catch up on schoolwork that he didn't do when he was very depressed. However, he seems to get stuck and then give up. Is there anything I can do to help?

As teens start to feel better, they often take on tasks that are too large. They then get discouraged because their efforts haven't gotten them very far.

Many teens don't want their teachers to know that they have been depressed, but if your son will agree, it might be helpful to meet with the principal or vice-principal to talk about reorganizing his work. Acknowledge that he can't just forget about the whole backlog, but see if something can be negotiated to cut back on the work and organize a schedule so that everything isn't due tomorrow.

If there is a course that he is extremely behind in, and that has a lot of work to be handed in, he might consider dropping the course and taking it in summer school.

Then sit down with him and help him break down larger assignments into smaller parts and design a reasonable work schedule with some built-in rewards (regular breaks, walks, food, going to an upbeat movie, phone calls to friends ...).

If he has a friend who is academically inclined, they might be able to work together. If they are in some of the same classes, the friend might be able to fill him in on some of what he missed. Even if your son wasn't physically absent from school, there is a good chance that he didn't hear much of what was going on in class when he was very depressed.

Remember that depression often involves feelings of hopelessness, so if you can help him get his work into a less daunting form you will be really helping him.

> My 16-year-old daughter just started in a group that her individual therapist recommended. She has gone to two sessions and seems very unenthusiastic. She came home the first week and said that the kids in the group were a bunch of losers, and yesterday she said that the leader was "really dumb" and made stupid rules. Should we take her out of the group?

I wouldn't take her out yet. It is common for depressed teens to be apathetic at the beginning of group therapy. She may be feeling so hopeless that she cannot believe that the group will help her. Or she may actually identify with other group members, which would mean that her put-downs of them could reflect her own negative self-perceptions. She may have gotten somewhat attached to feeling isolated and lonely or not want to make the attempt to be a member of the group for fear of failing.

The group leaders should be working hard at helping everybody feel included as a member of the group. This will include discussions and maybe some activities. It should not include bringing most of the group together by scapegoating one person in the group.

I would give this therapy at least three more sessions. If your daughter still wants to quit, ask her for permission to talk to one of the leaders about her decision (preferably with her) to discuss what is going on and find out what their perspective is. Hopefully you will be able to come to a consensus about whether she should continue.

My 17-year-old son has Down syndrome. He has seemed depressed to me lately, but our doctor said, "What do you expect? Other people his age are talking about going off to college, and he's being left behind. I'd be depressed too." But he has always been a happy, even-tempered person, and this is such a huge change. Are there different signs of depression in someone who is developmentally delayed? Should I be worried about him?

Trust your instincts on this. You know your son better than anyone else, and you've seen a big change in him. Although many people feel sad or angry when they realize that life is unfair, this doesn't mean they have an actual depression.

In general, the signs and symptoms of depression are similar for everyone. Changes in eating, weight and sleeping are common. Loss of interest in things that he enjoyed is another marker. One thing that is often seen in teens with a developmental delay is a loss of confidence. If he thinks he can't try to do new things or seems to be losing abilities, this is a real warning sign. He may ask for reassurance that he is doing okay or is capable of a task.

Your son might have difficulty expressing his feelings, especially complex ones like hopelessness. He may express these feelings with his behavior and may seem restless and irritable to you. He may snap at you and other family members. There may even be flares of anger, with destruction of things around him or self-harm, like banging his head on the wall.

Loss is often a trigger for depression. Have there been major changes in his life? A new school, talk of the possibility that he might move out, a death in the family (including pets) or a friend moving away could all be associated with the beginning of a depression. He may not have been able to talk about this loss. He may not even realize that it was upsetting to him. Although none of these things will cause a major depression, they can certainly contribute to one.

You should also try to figure out if he is being coerced into doing something that makes him feel uncomfortable. This could be an illegal activity (someone at school might be telling him to steal things) or a sexual activity.

Go back to your family doctor and explain your concerns again. Your son should have a physical exam and maybe some bloodwork to make sure that he does not have a medical problem. If he is on any type of medication, your doctor can check to see if mood changes are associated with taking it. Your family doctor may feel comfortable treating him or may want to refer him to a psychiatrist who has experience treating depression in teens with developmental delay. Psychotherapy can be helpful, especially therapies that use techniques developed for younger children, such as play and art therapy. Some cognitive behavioral techniques are also useful in this situation.

If your son is diagnosed with a depression, you can explain it so that he can understand where these feelings are coming from. Make sure he knows that it isn't his fault and that he will not always feel this way. He needs to hear that he is not crazy. Let him know that he will be able to do everything that he could do before, once he is feeling better. Encourage him to do what he can, but don't push him if he really feels unable.

Antidepressant medication may be needed. If so, it is important that side effects be explained so that your son won't think something terrible is happening to him. It may be hard for him to understand that it will take a while for medication to work, so you may want to circle a date in the calendar that is about four weeks after he starts and tell him the doctor thinks he will feel much better by then.

Hold off on any big changes in your lives. This is not the time to move or change schools. But don't try to protect him by not telling him about things that are happening. If there is a death in the family or an anticipated change, he should be included in any necessary planning.

Because depression is not a natural state and because he has a more upbeat temperament, you can assume that he will get better with treatment and move on with his life.

I have been depressed on and off for years. Now I am starting to notice signs of depression in my daughter. I feel terrible about this, and I am sure that living with me has made this happen to her. What can I do to help her?

The first thing you can do is to stop blaming yourself. Although your tendency to become depressed means that your daughter has a higher chance of developing depression (for genetic reasons), your living with her won't make her depressed, even though I am sure it is stressful for her.

You can decrease the stress on her by relying on other people for support in dealing with your depression. If you are using her as a counselor, support person or home care help, you are placing unreasonable expectations on her.

You can be a strong role model for her by getting help, taking your medication regularly and generally showing her that you are in charge and planning to recover. There will be days when this will require your best acting skills.

Get her to your family doctor or pediatrician for an assessment. You may be misinterpreting the normal mood swings of an adolescent because you are hypersensitive to signs of depression. You need an outside opinion. Do not give her your antidepressants.

Your daughter needs an adult source of support during

the times when you cannot provide it. This could be your partner, an aunt or uncle or a family friend.

I spend so much time worrying about my depressed 16-year-old that I feel as though my whole life revolves around him. I feel angry that I have to deal with this all the time, jealous of my friends' normal, healthy children and guilty that I feel this way. How can I better cope with someone who is depressed?

You are already doing one important thing, which is to acknowledge how you are feeling. Many parents feel angry with or about their depressed teens. In addition to feeling angry about the central role your son's depression is taking in your life, you may also feel angry if he seems to underutilize opportunities to get better or doesn't take his medication. As you are probably not telling him about this anger, you may find it coming out in arguments with him about other things. Although you shouldn't blame him for his depression, you can certainly tell him that it is sometimes frustrating. You can address specific issues (like missing medication) head-on, but in a non-accusatory way that will lead to a solution. Your son is probably also feeling angry and guilty about all this.

Parents often feel guilty about their teen's depression. We almost always blame ourselves for our children's problems, and you are also blaming yourself for how you feel. Rather than focusing on what you did wrong, concentrate on what you can do right. Stressful times like these are also opportunities to change.

It is difficult to live with someone who is depressed. His mood may drag you down, he requires more intensive parenting, his low energy may mean that he is contributing less to the running of the household and you may feel you have to be constantly vigilant about suicide.

Try to schedule some time for yourself. A walk with a friend, a game of chess, a movie or even a candlelit bath with some nice bath oil are all things you can do for yourself. If you keep a journal, this is not the time to ignore it. Time with your partner is also important, and make sure you are talking about things other than your son's predicament. Your other children also need your attention—you don't want them to get the idea that they must have a problem in order to get time with you. If you are having difficulty finding time for all this, prioritize the things that you feel you must do. (Is it really that important to vacuum every week?)

Increasing your alcohol or other drug intake is not a good way to cope with this situation. Your parenting skills will be negatively affected at a time when you need them the most. It is also poor role modeling.

Routines and rituals are important to families, and you should try to stick to them. Regular routines will reassure all your children that even if there are difficulties, your family is not falling apart. It will also give a sense of orderliness to a chaotic time. If your son won't participate in special occasions, you should continue with them and let him know he is free to change his mind. Even small, unofficial rituals are important, so continue with whatever you do for the last day of school, report-card day or the first snowfall of the year.

Maintaining a calm, ordered atmosphere also involves enforcing family rules. Some rules may need to be stretched because of your son's depression, but most rules (showing up for meals on time, doing household chores, being in by curfew or going to school every day) can and should be kept.

Remember that there is more to your son than his depression. Try to notice and acknowledge these other qualities as they show themselves. Speak positively about him both out loud and to yourself.

Try to find someone who has gone through this experience and get her practical tips. Not all of them will work for you, but some will, and they might be the things that get you through this in one piece.

Above all, remember that this is time limited. Your son *will* feel better, and life will improve for your whole family.

> *We live in a rural area. My son is on antidepressants and sees our family doctor regularly, but there aren't any other resources around here. Are there any Internet sites that would be helpful for him?*

There are many sites on the Internet, but not all of them are reliable. You might find information that is contradictory, so use your own judgment as best you can. While some sites are updated regularly, others are not.

Cyberisle (**www.cyberisle.org**) is a good site for teens that is loaded with health information. It also has a good tutorial to help teens assess web sites and to find valid information.

The Surgeon General of the United States has an online report on mental health (**www.sg.gov/library/mentalhealth**) that addresses depression. There are also a number of links on this site.

The best depression site with the most comprehensive links is Dr. Ivan's Depression Central (**www.psycom.ne/depression.central**). Two other helpful sites that you might want to check out are **www.mentalhealth.org** and **www.afsp.org**.

13. Depression and Society

Up to now, this book has dealt with depression from the point of view of depressed teens and their parents. But what about the society in which they live? Depression has social causes and consequences as well as private ones. Society also has a stake and a responsibility in the matter.

When parents set out to help their teens deal with depression, they usually prepare themselves to deal with the world of clinics, hospitals, therapists and doctors. But depression doesn't occur in a vacuum. It is not always just an individual medical condition; society has often had an influence in creating the conditions that allowed the depression to occur. And society may also have strong opinions about the depressed person.

Cultural and societal factors condition the way depression is viewed in a society. In some cultures depressed people may be seen as being possessed or as having done something wrong to feel this bad. At the other end of the spectrum are those who believe that mental illnesses are not really illnesses, but rather part of the normal range of human experience, and that diagnosing and treating these problems stigmatizes those involved and negates the normality of their experiences. Psychologist and drug guru Timothy Leary was at the extreme of this.

I take exception to this view of depression or any other mental illness. I've seen the pain some people are in, and I cannot accept any theory that calls it a normal phenomenon, and tells sufferers that they should simply tolerate it. On the other hand, when you read the DSM-IV (the *Diagnostic and Statistical Manual*, a publication that lists all psychiatric diagnoses) you may not think some of the conditions identified sound particularly disabling, or even very far from normal experience. For example, it seems to me that diagnoses like "oppositional defiant disorder" are being misused to label kids who are difficult and argumentative, but whose behavior is within the norm for their age.

Some artists feel that depression is the price they have to pay for a true awareness of the world around them, or that their depression leads them to insights they would not otherwise attain. People with bipolar illness are often much more creative during hypomanic phases (though, when frankly manic, their output may be large but of variable quality). If this is an idea your artist teen has, it might be hard for you to take action that he believes will thwart his creativity—you may be half convinced he is right! Society as a whole seems to accept mental illness as a part of the artistic process, but the truth is that most artists are mentally healthy.

The Politics of Depression Treatment

Treatment of depression can become a political issue, especially in systems where consumers pay directly for mental health services. When patients pay, therapists will often compete for the ones who have enough money, or sufficient insurance to cover their treatment. They may compete by making loud claims, insisting that their form of treatment is the only one that works. As you navigate this maze of claims, it is easy to become cynical about your child's value to these clinics or therapists. It is better to understand the system and look for ways to ensure equitable access to therapy for everyone who needs it, at all levels of society.

The unprepared parent may be tossed another political football in the possible association of suicide and homosexuality. This emotionally charged idea is used by the right to argue that gay people are clearly flawed, or that being gay is a horrible experience. It is used by the left to raise money for youth hotlines and other programs, even though suicide prevention is only one of many important services being offered.

There is evidence that both social class and gender are associated with the incidence of depression, but this does not mean that being female or poor causes depression. Poverty and gender are already arenas in which political battles are taking place. Empowerment through social action can help parents get beyond blaming themselves for conditions such as poverty that may have encouraged a depression.

Many social stressors correlate with depression, but there is no evidence that such stressors actually cause depression. Working to make life better for our own or for all teens is not going to make mental illnesses disappear, but relieving these stressors may mean that some teens with a genetic or biochemical vulnerability to depression will not develop a major depressive disorder.

This chapter looks not only at gender, sexual orientation and poverty and their possible links to depression, but also at resiliency—the ability of the teen to turn out mentally healthy despite these challenges. It is possible that many of the problems relating to depression and suicide will be solved politically, whether through funding prevention services that have been demonstrated to work or through people coming together in other projects to promote resiliency in our young people.

Gender and Depression

As discussed in Chapter 1, there is evidence that very young boys are more likely to become depressed than very young girls, but that this imbalance evens out in late childhood. In early to middle adolescence, we see an opposite split in the diagnosis of depression in boys and girls. By adulthood, women in Western countries are twice as likely as men to experience depression.

The evidence strongly shows that females are more likely to have depressive symptoms and diagnosable depression than males. For example, women are more likely than men to be admitted to psychiatric units suffering with depression. In large, population-based studies, depression has been shown to be more common in women. A three-year study in Edmonton, Alberta, showed that in any six-month period, 3.9 percent of women and only 2.5 percent of men met the criteria for a major depressive disorder. A Quebec study around the same time showed an even bigger difference, 3.7 percent for women and 1.7 percent for men.

Gender difference in the incidence of disease is found not only in depression but also in other illnesses as well, which indicates that there is a (still undiscovered) physical basis for the discrepancy. For instance, multiple sclerosis and systemic lupus erythematosus are both diseases that are more common in women.

A large Statistics Canada study published in the early

1980s looked at depressive symptoms rather than diagnoses. Women were twice as likely to report frequent symptoms of depression and anxiety than men. One American study showed that in addition to the expected gender differences, women of color, those living in poverty and those who were less educated were more likely to be depressed. Women are more likely to earn low wages than men with the same qualifications and to be supporting children on their own, thus making it more likely that they will live in poverty. Poorly performed studies looking at gender differences in depression often don't control for income and expenses and thus get inaccurate results.

Just as there is probably no single cause for depression, it is unlikely that any single factor is responsible for the gender differences that have been identified in many studies. A combination of biological and societal factors are probably involved.

Biological Factors

GENETICS

Genetic factors are sometimes suggested as the cause of the gender gap in depression and other illnesses, but this theory has not been pinned down. In general, diseases carried on the X chromosome (of which women have two and men one) tend to be more common in men. Many diseases are "recessive," that is, if one of a pair of chromosomes has the gene for an illness and the other has a healthy gene, the healthy one prevails. Because the X chromosome in women is paired, it usually takes two unhealthy genes to cause a disease, but because men have one X and one Y, it only takes one gene to cause a disease. It is therefore unlikely that an abnormal gene on the X chromosome is the cause of an increased rate of depression in women.

HORMONES

Similarly, differences between males and females are often attributed to hormones. But men and women have the same hormones—there is no hormone that is strictly male or female. There are gender differences in the ratios and amounts of the hormones usually referred to as sex hormones. Hormone theories of depression are appealing because children have low levels of sex hormones, and there are no gender differences in rates of depression in older children. Researchers in this area have mainly looked at types of depression thought to be associated with hormone fluctuations (premenstrual syndrome [PMS], postpartum depression and depression associated with menopause) rather than looking at hormone levels in women with depressions not associated with these states. However, a lot of data shows that increasing rates of depression in teens are associated with age rather than with the stage of puberty that has been reached, arguing against a direct link to hormone levels.

PMS is a problem that is difficult to research, as everyone "knows" that girls and women get depressed or crabby before their menstrual periods. Therefore, asking people to report moods after the fact, or doing PMS research when the women in the study know that it is about PMS, leads to problems. When Canadian university students (in two studies) were asked to make a note of their daily mood, they were just as likely to report depressed feelings after their periods or in the middle of their cycle as they were just before their periods. When they were asked to look back and report on their mood at different stages in their last cycle, they recalled having more unpleasant feelings during their premenstrual phase, although their daily records didn't support this recollection. Other studies that have looked at large groups of women may have missed a smaller group who do have mood changes associated with their cycles.

As noted in Chapter 1, the postpartum period (after a baby is born) is full of changes and stressors that could affect mood; hormone fluctuations are just one of many factors. Again, the research is inconclusive and if small numbers of women suffer from significant depressions after childbirth due to changes in hormones, it could be difficult to identify them in large studies in which most women did well.

Researchers have not been able to show an increase in depression around the time of natural menopause. In fact, peak rates of depression occur before this time, which would make sense if higher levels of hormone are associated with depression, as menopause is associated with lower levels of hormones. However, there are many social factors that could explain lower levels of depression in post-menopausal women, including lack of anxiety about unwanted pregnancy, decreased child care responsibilities and perhaps more financial stability at this time of life.

Societal Factors

VIOLENCE

The high incidence of violence against girls and women may also contribute to gender differences in depression. Parents are often unaware that their daughter is in an abusive relationship. An early warning sign is a boyfriend who seems very possessive. Abusive boyfriends try to cut a girl off from her other friends early in the relationship and tend to be suspicious of any interaction the girl has with another boy. They start making increasingly critical remarks about her appearance, the way she talks, her interests. Physical violence may start with a very tight grip on her arm or a similar escalation of a normal, affectionate gesture. Although depression isn't the most common result of abuse (fear, lowered self-esteem and anger are more prevalent), it is reported as an effect of the abuse in about 10 to 15 percent of abused girls and women.

Girls are not abused just by boyfriends. Emotional, physical and sexual abuse are actually more likely to take place in the home. One study showed that depressed adult women were much more likely to have been abused as children than those who weren't depressed, and that they were more likely to have been abused more frequently, more severely and in several ways.

SOCIAL EXPECTATIONS

Expectations placed on women may be another factor that contributes to gender differences in depression. Despite feminism and the many changes that have occurred in our society, girls still often feel that they have to meet a high standard of appearance, have to know how to massage male egos and, at the same time, prepare for careers and a fast-track life. We expect young women to grow up and become mothers, but we don't prepare them for this job, and the supports needed to do it well are not consistently in place. Women with young children, especially women without access to child care or support from a spouse, are more likely to be depressed than men with young children or women without children.

It may be that a biological predisposition to depression is equally common in males and females, but that events that trigger depression are more likely to happen to adolescent girls than boys. For example, girls in early adolescence may feel a large sense of loss as physical development transforms their bodies from being strong and agile to bodies that seem more cumbersome. Boys, on the other hand, find their bodies becoming stronger and more muscular.

Conversely, it may be that there are different causes for

depression in males and females and that these underlying factors occur equally in late childhood, but that female causative factors occur more frequently in adolescence than male factors do.

Our expectations of girls and boys diverge greatly in adolescence. Our role expectations of girls may be particularly stressful. We assume that girls will be nicer, more helpful, more self-sacrificing, more socially focused and more cooperative. A girl who does not fit this mold and who has poor coping and problem-solving techniques may have an increased rate of depression.

Girls' experience of depression seems to be different from boys'. Studies have shown that depressed girls are more likely to say that they feel unattractive and want to lose weight. Girls in our culture often link their self-worth to others' perceptions of them, or what they think are others' perceptions. If a teen's body isn't the size and shape that she believes is fashionable, she may see herself as worthless and be more vulnerable to depression.

Aboriginal Suicide

Young native people are committing suicide at tragically high rates around the world. In Canada, aboriginal youth kill themselves at a rate that is five times the national average for their age group.

As with other youth, young First Nations males and females attempt suicide at the same rates, but young men are much more likely to die as they use more violent means. Rates of gun ownership are high in many native communities.

Many aspects of modern aboriginal communities have been linked to these high rates of suicide, including sexual abuse, alcohol and substance abuse, high rates of unemployment and the lack of open discussion in many communities about suicide and depression. In addition, supports such as traditional customs that can form a strong framework for teens and cohesive families who follow these traditions have been systematically weakened over the past several hundred years.

Relocation has had a major effect on many communities. Many moves have been to small areas that lack hunting and fishing grounds. As the traditional economy of a community is eroded, young people have a hard time finding a way to be productive, contributing members of the community. The resulting loss of self-esteem and decreased feelings of self-worth are important contributors to feelings of hopelessness.

Teens in many of these communities face poverty, lack of advanced education, joblessness, a high risk of substance abuse and a lack of recreational opportunities.

Young native people today have been raised by parents and grandparents who have been severely affected by the residential schooling that they received as children. These kids were removed from their communities and exiled to schools where they were punished for speaking their languages, made to dress like white people and often physically and sexually abused. These parents were ripped from their communities, losing their sense of place in the world. They lost strong traditions that could have given them security, and identity, harmony and a feeling of belonging. The residential schools punched a large hole into all the communities affected, and the hole cannot be repaired easily.

Many communities are starting to open the dialog about teen suicide and to use a number of innovative approaches to try to solve this problem. These solutions are being shared at conferences and on the Internet. All workable ideas will be based on addressing more than the issue of suicide.

Poverty and Depression

I once heard someone say that poor children don't get depressed, they just get hungry. Hunger can certainly mimic many signs of depression, besides having negative effects on many body systems. In younger children, brain development can be affected by malnutrition. In teens, the long-term effects of hunger would include not only that kind of damage, but also a feeling of being chronically deprived, with the poor self-esteem that could result. When these brain effects already exist, and an acutely starved state is added to the mix, it isn't surprising that these teens might show many signs of depression, including looking sad, losing weight, and having poor concentration, low energy and sleep problems. A good school breakfast and lunch program would go a long way to help with this problem and might even help a teen with a true depression, as the extra energy might give her the boost she needs to seek help.

Even with nutritional supplements, the higher incidence of depression among teens living in poverty would not disappear. Although there is some conflicting evidence, most studies that have looked at poverty and emotional problems in children and youth have shown a strong correlation between these conditions, especially at the lowest income levels. This does not mean that poverty causes depression, just that poverty and depression are more likely to occur together than depression and wealth.

People who live in poverty often feel powerless. Their inability to provide for their children, to control their environment and to engage in meaningful work can be deeply discouraging. Marginalized from mainstream culture, they may feel irrelevant to the functioning of society, stigmatized and unimportant.

Poorer neighborhoods are more crowded, have less public space (such as parks or pedestrian malls) and have higher levels of substance abuse and violence. Living in such an environment increases feelings of hopelessness and powerlessness, and produces a high level of chronic stress in people who do not have the means to relieve stress that are available to middle- and upper-class families. Social class goes beyond issues of poverty and wealth. Children who grow up knowing that they don't belong to the middle class often get the message from their classmates, the media, teachers and others that they aren't as good as other kids.

Children and teens whose mothers have a low level of education are more likely to experience psychiatric problems, including depression and problems at school. Working-class women are less likely than middle- and upper-class women to have high levels of education.

There is a link between adversity and depression in children and adolescents. Teens from lower socioeconomic classes often face subtle discrimination at school, fewer extracurricular opportunities and chronic stress, all of which could be classified as adversity. Many researchers have shown a strong link between feelings of social inferiority, powerlessness, lack of control and poor physical and mental health.

Depression is associated with poverty, and the two also have a reverse relationship: where there is depression, poverty may be found. A parent who is depressed may lose his job, or only be able to function at a level far below his potential, and therefore end up poor. The child has many stressors: a change in social class and economic situation, a depressed mother or father and perhaps a genetic predisposition to depression.

People from higher social classes have grown up learning how to access what they need and feeling that they deserve what they need. Even when services are free, poorer parents and teens may not know how to get them, may not be aware that they exist, may not be able to afford transportation to get to them and may lack (even the literacy) skills needed to find out about them.

Gay Teens

I have already discussed the link between suicide and gay teens. There is much less evidence regarding depression and gay teens, but it is clear that having a minority sexual orientation can be stressful for teens. It is clear to young people that our society is still intolerant of gay people in a number of ways. Human rights protection varies between jurisdictions. The murder of gay student Matthew Shepard on October 12, 1998, in Wyoming, made it clear that homophobia can be fatal.

Parents have an opportunity to help young gays and lesbians in a number of ways. For example, they can speak with teens about homophobia, they can support human rights legislation and they can support the inclusion of information about homosexuality in sexual health classes.

Larger cities have gay youth phone lines and special school programs for young people who have been forced to leave mainstream schools because of homophobia. These special programs would certainly appreciate your volunteer hours, money and any other donations.

Parents and Friends of Lesbians and Gays (PFLAG) is an organization with chapters throughout the United States and Canada. Your local group would be glad to give you suggestions about what can be done to help the lesbian and gay teens in your area.

What Protects Kids from Developing Depression?

In Chapter 2, I discussed Jules, a teen who seemed to have the whole deck stacked against him but who was happy and active. Jules was resilient—he had the quality that allowed him to live in a difficult situation and come through healthy and confident. Resilience protects from risk. It is not a single entity, but is a number of factors that may happily come together in an otherwise at-risk teen.

We would like to be able to teach resilience, but some of the factors that promote resilience seem to be inherent in a teen's makeup, such as a calm, optimistic, naturally autonomous temperament, good social skills and a genetic predisposition to good mental health.

Although levels of social stress may be difficult or impossible to change, parents who have a positive perspective and who can help their children deal with stress can greatly enhance resilience. Even a close relationship to parents in the absence of this positive outlook confers quite a bit of protection.

Some things that promote resilience seem to happen by chance, such as an opportunity to go on a school exchange where the teen talks with someone or learns something that challenges her or changes the direction she is taking. Having a good relationship with an adult who can become a mentor can be crucial. Resilient teens feel cared for by at least one person. They know that others will support them, and challenge them with high expectations. This person may be related to them, but could also be a neighbor, teacher, community worker, guidance counselor, coach or family friend. Through involvement in teams or clubs, teens may find these adult mentors, and also benefit from the other advantages of belonging to a structured group: increased social competence, relief from boredom, a chance to learn new skills and an acceptable outlet for aggression.

Relationships with friends are extremely important to teens. They promote resilience by giving the teen someone with whom they can share feelings and ideas and practice relational problem solving. Friendships, if they are on an equal footing, increase self-esteem and promote independence.

Teens whose parents and other mentors have imbued them with the sense that their lives have meaning, be it a religious, political, intellectual or other meaning, and that they can overcome adversity and seek out the social supports they need, are more resilient than those who have not developed these attitudes. All of these teens have a base of self-confidence and self-esteem.

For children and teens who live with two parents, the quality of that relationship has an impact on their resilience. Parents who communicate well and who get along are more able to be consistent and calm in their parenting, promoting impulse control and positive problem solving in their children. Conversely, parental discord decreases the chance of either partner working as part of a parenting team. The level of tension rises and, if violence ensues, the teen is more likely to become aggressive in his own relationships or engage in other antisocial behavior. If the parents split up, there is an increased chance that the children will be raised in poverty, with all the problems that result.

An authoritative parenting style (what Barbara Coloroso, the parenting guru, refers to as "backbone" parents) with consistency, high but reasonable expectations and an attunement to the child's emotional needs (showing itself as high levels of reciprocal respect rather than a top-down model) is also associated with resilience. These parents do not avoid confrontations, but deal with them in a non-coercive manner.

Hopelessness is often a striking part of depression. Teens who have learned that they can solve problems, recover from adversity and even triumph over defeat are in general more resilient and probably have some specific protection against depression.

Political Action to Prevent Suicide

Many factors that increase suicidal risk for teens are also the targets of political activism. One example is antipoverty work. Teens who grow up with low family incomes are at increased risk of killing themselves. If we work to eradicate poverty, both by changing the system and by creating programs to empower families, giving them the tools they need to reduce the consequences of poverty, there might be a corresponding reduction in teen suicides and other mental health problems.

Mental health activism can also be important. Although some of the more extreme groups in this area feel that psychiatric diagnosis and treatment are used to control people not help them, other, less doctrinaire groups work to get appropriate mental health services to the people who need them, advocate for people in the system and support broad prevention activities. This work is important because we know that mentally ill teens, especially those with serious problems such as bipolar disorder and schizophrenia, can have greatly improved long-term outcomes if they are treated early in their illness. In addition, young teens whose parents have psychiatric problems are at increased risk of suicide, so if treatment is more accessible to parents it is likely that the teens would also benefit. Family dysfunction is also linked with teen suicide, and family mental health programs that help families work together effectively may also, hopefully, prevent some suicides.

Suicide prevention activities directed at teens include hotlines and school-based programs. Hotlines seem to be helpful for females; there isn't any evidence that they reduce suicide rates for males, but this may be because males don't tend to use these services.

The value of school programs is also limited; teens at highest risk of suicide are probably among those most likely to be away from school on any given day. In addition, many of these programs stress that teens who kill themselves are not mentally ill. The assumption behind this approach is that teens think only "crazy people" commit suicide, and might not identify peers or themselves as being at risk when they are depressed, because they are not crazy.

There seems to be a hope that the stigma of suicide will be decreased if it is not linked to mental illness, which could result in teens being more willing to identify themselves as suicidal and ask for help. The designers of these programs seem to think that teens can understand only the immediate precipitants of suicide, usually interpersonal stress, and that the idea of long-term underlying factors is too complicated for them.

I don't think that a prevention program should be based on misleading statements, even if there seem to be good reasons for sugar-coating the truth. It makes sense that providing accurate information would work better, in addition to the ethical reasons for doing so. Also, if these programs did succeed in removing the stigma from suicide the result might actually make committing suicide seem more acceptable. If you want to become involved in a suicide prevention program directed to teens, find one that is honest, has a proven track record and feels right to you.

For people who are perhaps less political, but who would like to work to prevent suicide in teens, we know that substance use (most often alcohol) plays an important role in teen suicide. Many teens who try to kill themselves have been drinking or taking other drugs at the time. After depression, ongoing substance abuse is one of the most common underlying mental health problems in teens who kill themselves. Teens who have parents who drink to excess are also at higher risk of suicide. So, supporting programs that provide effective treatment to teens and adults could have an impact on teen suicides. Most prevention programs have never been adequately evaluated to see if they really are effective in preventing teens from getting involved with alcohol and drugs. If you can find one that has been shown to work, it would be worth supporting.

With the huge role that firearms play in adolescent suicide, especially in the United States, working for gun control could also have a positive impact on suicide rates. This can be depressing work, as there is a well-mobilized and highly funded opposition to any control of gun ownership or use, but I believe that the movement to restrict access to guns can be successful.

Although the data about gay teens and suicide is still not strong, it does seem clear that young gays and lesbians are more likely to attempt suicide than other teens. Supporting gay youth hotlines, support groups, educational programs and other activities aimed at helping these often isolated young people may prevent suicide attempts. As with all other efforts, these programs should try to build in an evaluative component so that their efficacy can be determined.

Helping young people become involved in political action can have a preventative effect. These activities can help teens feel empowered and hopeful. As they focus on other people's problems, their own are kept in perspective. Teens can be encouraged to join environmental or other groups. Adults can help by providing operational advice (how to get appointments with politicians; how to organize a phone tree, meeting or demonstration), by providing seed money or helping with a fundraiser, or by providing meeting space, file cabinets, fabric for banners or refreshments for meetings.

While helping your depressed teen, you are unlikely to have the time or energy to consider the societal roots of her problem, or to become involved in political action, but as things improve, these may be issues that become important to you, or are at least interesting to think about.

There are many ways in which depression is a social issue. Although the people most profoundly affected by a teen's depression are herself and her family, the condition has wider implications. People who are depressed may be less productive at work or school. Their care incurs costs to them and to society. At the simplest level, they cannot contribute to society as fully as when they are well.

Appendix:
Types of
Psychotherapy

The general issues concerning psychotherapy were discussed in Chapter 5. Most of the many different types of psychotherapy have not yet been systematically tested in teens.

Although the evidence for the usefulness of psychotherapy in depressed teens is lacking, most doctors recommend psychotherapy in depressed teens, usually in conjunction with medication. The evidence clearly shows that medication works for teens, but, at the very least, we need to support teens while they are waiting for the medication to work and to help them deal with or avoid factors that lead to the depression. Biologic risk for depression probably exists in many teens who do not become depressed, so looking at the factors that might have triggered a depression is important, not only to improve present functioning, but also to prevent future bouts of depression.

Psychodynamically Oriented Therapy

A psychodynamic approach is what most of us think of as "therapy." It is based on the idea that our childhood experiences, even those we don't remember, have a profound effect on us and unconsciously motivate our feelings and how we act. Internal conflicts that arise from these early experiences are reflected in the therapeutic sessions and in the teen's behavior.

We all have a picture of the movie psychoanalyst whose clients lie on a couch free-associating several times a week for many years while the therapist says, "Yah," or "Und does zat remind you uf your mother?" This is not an accurate picture of psychoanalysis (which isn't often used for depressed teens anyway). Psychodynamically oriented therapists are active partners in therapy, developing a relationship, discussing events and issues in the teen's life, helping her identify contradictions and themes and asking questions that help her express and identify her feelings.

Psychodynamic therapists think it is important to pay attention to the teen's feelings about the therapist and the therapist's feelings about the teen. Examination of these feelings gives information that might not be available otherwise.

Early in the process, the therapist focuses on developing a "therapeutic alliance" with the teen. This not only creates a basis for further therapeutic work, but also is an end unto itself. It creates a model for the teen for a type of relationship where there is trust and recognition of her feelings. The existence of this alliance may boost self-confidence and self-esteem.

Psychodynamic therapies are particularly useful for teens who are "insight oriented" and willing to express themselves, but can also be used in others, often with play or art techniques. These therapies tend to take longer than some other approaches.

The therapy does not delve into the past only, but deals with present issues, seeing the depression as a part of the teen's life. The therapist explores how the teen functions with others, what she sees as her role in relationships and how she deals with losses in this context, while paying attention to mood and past experiences.

There are many types of psychodynamically oriented therapy, including interpersonal therapy and self-in-relation therapy (which combines psychodynamic, interpersonal and feminist theories).

Cognitive-Behavior Therapy

Like psychodynamically oriented therapy, cognitive-behavior therapy, initially developed by Drs. Albert Ellis and Aaron Beck, is also based on talking, on exploring current problems and with ways that people think. Based on the idea that moods are created by thoughts, it explores thinking patterns, especially negative ones. These can include thinking that dismisses positive experiences or translates them into negative ones, seeing oneself as responsible for negative experiences and dwelling on negative aspects of life. Many of these thoughts are considered to be automatic—that is, they are a quick response to a stimulus and not under conscious control. The therapist helps the teen to look at these thoughts, to find typical ways that she reacts to issues in her life and to discover any negative assumptions and misperceptions she may have. The therapist and teen together then try to find ways to view life differently or to use different tactics when dealing with problems.

The cognitive therapist recognizes that every teen is different and helps each one explore her individual thinking patterns. As with almost all types of therapy, the cognitive approach involves a partnership between the teen and the therapist.

A teen in an early stage of cognitive development may have difficulty identifying his thoughts and developing alternative ways of looking at things, as the practice of thinking about thinking may be difficult for someone who is not yet using much abstract reasoning. However, a cognitive therapist may be able to teach specific reasoning skills as part of therapy. The emphasis on thoughts as a way to deal with feelings may appeal to some adolescents. Another appealing aspect to teens of this type of therapy is that the goals of each therapy session are clearly set out at the beginning. This "agenda" can help a teen who is having difficulty concentrating to focus on specific issues. He may feel encouraged when the therapist expresses a clear idea of where the therapy is going. Teens are active participants in designing the agenda, setting priorities and setting goals.

Early stages of cognitive therapy are similar to other types, in that much of the work focuses on developing a therapeutic alliance and on identifying issues. Later on, the identification of thought processes becomes key, with problem-solving leading to changes in these processes by looking at the validity of the thought, by identifying alternative perspectives and by replacing negative thoughts. The teen then has the opportunity to practice his new skills outside of therapy and to discuss the outcomes with the therapist. When difficulties arise out of a particular situation or conflict with others, this approach can help the teen to approach these difficulties in a positive fashion.

Cognitive therapists often give teens "homework." It is a good idea for parents to stay out of this and to avoid enforcing the performance of this work or delving into the assignment. You may want to ask your teen if she would like a reminder at some point in the week, but one reminder would be the maximum.

When there is a clear-cut diagnosis of depression, this type of therapy is fairly short-term. It gives teens a chance to practice new behaviors and makes them more aware of their ability to control their lives. It is not useful with very disturbed teens or with those who cannot think clearly for other reasons.

Short-term (three to five months) cognitive therapy has been found to be effective in up to about 60 percent of depressed people (not necessarily teens). Studies have shown that it has a low relapse rate; that is, after this type of therapy, people are less likely to have another depression than those treated in other ways. Cognitive therapy can be offered individually, in groups or in families.

Behavior Modification Therapy

Behavior modification therapy is often useful in the treatment of those with anxiety, with substance abuse problems or with other dependencies. On its own, it is not very useful for depression.

Based on the work of physiologist Ivan Pavlov and those who developed his ideas, this therapy uses ideas about learning, also called conditioning. In this theory, all behavior is a learned response to a stimulus. Two kinds of learning are identified: respondent and operant. Respondent conditioning involves a neutral stimulus, such as the sound of a bell, being paired with something that causes a response motivated by a biological need, such as hunger. After a number of exposures, the animal responds to the neutral stimulus alone with the biological or behavioral response it had to the other stimulus.

Operant conditioning is more complicated. It involves the consequences of actions. A behavior that is originally random will be repeated if consistently reinforced or rewarded, or it will be stopped if it is punished or otherwise discouraged. This is one of the ways we teach our children to be polite—by complimenting them when they say please or thank you, and by denying requests that are not accompanied by a "please."

Behavior theorists would say that depression is a result of poor reinforcement for actions. If there are no rewards, the teen becomes withdrawn. He may get attention because of this withdrawal, positively reinforcing passivity. The therapist helps the teen learn to find the inherent rewards in life and uses techniques to help him stop negative thoughts.

A therapist who uses only behavior therapy regards feelings (and to some extent, thoughts) as irrelevant and deals only with behavior, which may make a teen feel dehumanized. Behavior therapy can be helpful in treating phobias or in helping someone to quit smoking.

Some behavior modification techniques can be used with other therapeutic approaches. Relaxation exercises, modeling of appropriate behavior and reinforcement or rewarding of positive behavior all fit under the umbrella of behavior therapy.

Supportive Therapy

Many family doctors and nurses offer counseling, also known as supportive therapy. The therapist listens to the teen's problems, reassures her that she is normal, gives suggestions about other ways to handle situations and guidance about problem solving. Supportive therapy can help a teen who has been functioning well but who develops depressed feelings in response to a life event. It can also be helpful as an accompaniment to antidepressant medication.

Other Therapies

There are a number of other therapeutic approaches that don't really fit into any of the above categories. Solution-focused therapy is a brief process that looks at the immediate problems and deals with them in a fairly pragmatic way. Narrative therapy is an offshoot of communications theory that uses storytelling as a major tool. Jungian therapy focuses on the teen reaching his personal potential as an individual through a number of techniques, including a focus on the spiritual dimension. Two others are Gestalt and Adlerian therapy.

Index